Women Leaders
of Nations

Other Books in the History Makers Series:

Women Leaders of Nations

By Don Nardo

Lucent Books
P.O. Box 289011, San Diego, CA 92198-9011

Library of Congress Cataloging-in-Publication Data

Nardo, Don, 1947–
      Women leaders of nations / by Don Nardo.
            p.   cm. — (History makers)
      Includes bibliographical references and index.
      Summary: Discusses some notable female leaders of history, including
Cleopatra, Queen Victoria, and Golda Meir.
      ISBN 1-56006-397-1 (lib. : alk. paper)
      1. Heads of state—Biography—Juvenile literature.   2. Women in
Politics—Biography—Juvenile literature.   3. Leadership—Juvenile litera-
ture. [1. Kings, queens, rulers, etc. 2. Heads of state. 3. Women—
Biography.] I. Title.   II. Series.
D107.3.N37   1999
920.72'088'351—dc21   98-35810
[B]   CIP
                                                                                            AC

Copyright 1999 by Lucent Books, Inc.
P.O. Box 289011, San Diego, California 92198-9011

Printed in the U.S.A.

CONTENTS

FOREWORD

The literary form most often referred to as "multiple biography" was perfected in the first century A.D. by Plutarch, a perceptive and talented moralist and historian who hailed from the small town of Chaeronea in central Greece. His most famous work, *Parallel Lives*, consists of a long series of biographies of noteworthy ancient Greek and Roman statesmen and military leaders. Frequently, Plutarch compares a famous Greek to a famous Roman, pointing out similarities in personality and achievements. These expertly constructed and very readable tracts provided later historians and others, including playwrights like Shakespeare, with priceless information about prominent ancient personages and also inspired new generations of writers to tackle the multiple biography genre.

The Lucent History Makers series proudly carries on the venerable tradition handed down from Plutarch. Each volume in the series consists of a set of six to eight biographies of important and influential historical figures who were linked together by a common factor. In *Rulers of Ancient Rome*, for example, all the figures were generals, consuls, or emperors of either the Roman Republic or Empire; while the subjects of *Fighters Against American Slavery*, though they lived in different places and times, all shared the same goal, namely the eradication of human servitude. Mindful that politicians and military leaders are not (and never have been) the only people who shape the course of history, the editors of the series have also included representatives from a wide range of endeavors, including scientists, artists, writers, philosophers, religious leaders, and sports figures.

Each book is intended to give a range of figures—some well known, others less known; some who made a great impact on history, others who made only a small impact. For instance, by making Columbus's initial voyage possible, Spain's Queen Isabella I, featured in *Women Leaders of Nations*, helped to open up the New World to exploration and exploitation by the European powers. Unarguably, therefore, she made a major contribution to a series of events that had momentous consequences for the entire world. By contrast, Catherine II, the eighteenth-century Russian queen, and Golda Meir, the modern Israeli prime minister, did not play roles of global impact; however, their policies and actions significantly influenced the historical development of both their own countries and their regional neighbors. Regardless of their relative importance in the greater historical scheme, all of the figures chronicled in the History Makers series made contributions to posterity; and their public achievements, as well as what is known about their private lives, are presented and evaluated in light of the most recent scholarship.

In addition, each volume in the series is documented and substantiated by a wide array of primary and secondary source quotations. The primary source quotes enliven the text by presenting eyewitness views of the times and culture in which each history maker lived; while the secondary source quotes, taken from the works of respected modern scholars, offer expert elaboration and/ or critical commentary. Each quote is footnoted, demonstrating to the reader exactly where biographers find their information. The footnotes also provide the reader with the means of conducting additional research. Finally, to further guide and illuminate readers, each volume in the series features photographs, a chronology, two bibliographies, and a comprehensive index.

The History Makers series provides both students engaged in research and more casual readers with informative, enlightening, and entertaining overviews of individuals from a variety of circumstances, professions, and backgrounds. No doubt all of them, whether loved or hated, benevolent or cruel, constructive or destructive, will remain endlessly fascinating to each new generation seeking to identify the forces that shaped their world.

"Singular Exceptions" in a Man's World

"It was certainly a thing most marvelous," exclaimed the fifteenth-century Spanish historian Hernando del Pulgar, "that what many men and great lords did not manage to do in many years, a single woman did in a short time through work and governance."[1] Pulgar's statement referred to Queen Isabella I, who ruled the Spanish kingdom of Castile in the late 1400s. But it could just as appropriately have described anyone on the short but impressive list of capable women who have wielded the enormous political and military power that comes with leading a nation.

That so few women have held such formidable positions is hardly surprising. Throughout most of human history, the corridors of state power were reserved mainly for men. In nearly all societies, women were seen as either less intelligent than men or inherently lacking the various special qualities and talents needed to govern, or both. Generally, young women were encouraged to find happiness in raising children and faithfully supporting the lofty goals and ambitions of their fathers, husbands, brothers, and sons; for a woman to express lofty goals and ambitions of her own was usually viewed as improper, unnatural, or even dangerous. The sixteenth-century Scottish religious reformer John Knox spoke for a majority of men in history when he said:

> To promote a women to bear rule, superiority, dominion, or empire above any realm, nation, or city is repugnant to Nature, contumely [contemptible] to God, a thing most contrarious to His revealed will and approved ordinance; and finally it is the subversion of good order, of all equity and justice. . . . For who can deny but it is repugnant to Nature that the blind shall be appointed to lead and conduct such as do see? . . . Woman in her greatest perfection was made to serve and obey man, not to rule and command him.[2]

Faced with this harsh and all too common male attitude, remarks historian Vicki Leon, "lying low would have seemed to be a wise course" for women to follow. And as a rule "many women did just that, for centuries."[3]

The eight subjects of this volume are perhaps the most famous of the handful of exceptions to this rule. Thanks to varying circumstances, almost always unusual and fortuitous, each challenged the male-dominated status quo, took charge of a nation-state and its people, and governed both firmly and effectively. The first, Cleopatra (ca. 69–30 B.C.), remains not only the most famous female national leader of ancient times but also the archetype, or most enduring model and symbol, of all women leaders. As ruler of Egypt, one of the oldest and most prestigious of nations, Cleopatra long held her own among the strong male leaders of her day, including the legendary Julius Caesar. A nineteenth-century French writer called her "the most complete woman ever to have existed, the most womanly woman and the most queenly queen, a person to be wondered at, to whom the poets have been able to add nothing, and whom dreamers find always at the end of their dreams."[4]

Egypt's Cleopatra VII, last ruler of the Greek Ptolemaic dynasty, had the audacity to challenge some of the most powerful men in her world.

From Absolutism to Democracy

Later powerful women invariably had to suffer comparison with the legendary Cleopatra. This is manifestly unfair; over the centuries her deeds, though impressive, have been exaggerated, and her personal charms and traits, though admirable, have been grossly sensationalized and romanticized. Isabella (1451–1504), who helped drive the Moors out of Spain and supported Columbus's early ventures, was undoubtedly just as charming and capable. And England's Elizabeth I (1533–1603), though perhaps not as charming as the first two (she was both vain and demanding), was every bit their equal in politics and war. A strong supporter of the arts and a wise promoter of trade and mercantilism, she also stood up to and defeated the infamous Spanish Armada, a vast invasion force bent on removing her from power. Catherine

II (1729–1796), often called "the Great," absolute ruler of Russia's huge empire, had much in common with Elizabeth. The Russian queen (who was actually Polish by birth), like her English counterpart, vigorously promoted the arts and foreign trade. Catherine also successfully led her nation in war, significantly expanding her empire at the expense of the Turks and Poles.

Cleopatra, Isabella, Elizabeth, and Catherine all had in common their absolutism. That is, each wielded the complete (or nearly complete) power of life and death over her subjects that was a traditional, often hereditary, and largely accepted right of monarchs in premodern times. By contrast, the other four women covered in this volume, though tough, effective leaders, came to power in modern democratic societies. So each was limited, to one degree or another, by the legal and political constraints that democracies place on their public servants. Queen Victoria (1819–1901) and Prime Minister Margaret Thatcher (1925–) often had to bend to the will of the British Parliament, for instance. And Israel's prime minister Golda Meir (1898–1978) and Pakistan's prime minister Benazir Bhutto (1953–) were similarly limited by the authority of their own national legislatures.

The eighteenth-century Russian empress Catherine the Great, as she appeared toward the end of her long reign.

Little Has Changed

Yet all four of these talented women proved to be strong and resourceful leaders. Under Victoria, the longest reigning monarch in British history, Britain consolidated its world empire; a century later, having lost most of that empire, Britain proved it was still a power to be reckoned with when (in 1982), led by Thatcher, it defeated Argentina in a dispute over the Falkland Islands. Meir led her own nation to victory in a 1973 war against Israel's Arab neighbors (although she was later criticized for the high number of Israeli casualties). And Bhutto is credited with reinstating democracy in Pakistan after that country had fallen into dictatorship.

Despite these and other accomplishments made by women leaders over the centuries, the acquisition of high political position by a woman is overall a rare occurrence. The great eighteenth-century English historian Edward Gibbon remarked that it is a "singular exception" when "a woman is . . . acknowledged the absolute sovereign of a great kingdom, in which she would [otherwise] be deemed incapable of exercising the smallest employment, civil, or military."[5] That the vast majority of today's nations, including the United States, have never had a woman president, prime minister, or commander in chief shows that little has changed since Gibbon's time. Perhaps some day women will run nations as often as men do, rendering his phrase obsolete. Only then will leaders like Cleopatra, Isabella, and Benazir Bhutto be judged as men have al-

Former British prime minister Margaret Thatcher, who led her nation in its 1982 recovery of the Falkland Islands.

ways been and deemed exceptional, not because they have achieved so much despite their gender, but solely on the merits of those achievements.

CHAPTER 1

Warrior Women Through the Ages

The identity of the first woman who ever actually ruled a nation or a people on her own, without the aid or guidance of a man, is forever lost in the mists of time. It is likely that such powerful women, even if they were rare, existed very early in the human saga. After all, the classical Greeks (fifth century B.C.) had legends about them that were already extremely old; and legends, however exaggerated and distorted, are often based on fact.

Warrior Women of the Steppes

The Greek tales about the Amazons, the fabulous ancient tribe of warrior women, is a case in point. Early Greek myths frequently featured Greek men fighting Amazons, as in the story of how an army of Amazons landed at Marathon, northeast of Athens, threatening the city but ultimately suffering defeat at the hands of Athenian troops. The Greeks referred to such warfare with the warrior women as *Amazonomachy,* which became a common theme depicted in Greek literature, sculpture, and painting. Some of the sculptures carved into the Parthenon (the temple of the goddess Athena erected atop the Athenian Acropolis in the 430s B.C.), for example, showed battles with Amazons.[6]

The location of the Amazons' homeland varied from one myth to another, but the areas most often cited were the wild and little-known steppes lying west and north of the Black Sea. The Greek historian Herodotus (often called "the Father of History") traveled through some of these areas circa 450 B.C. The local people, seminomadic horsemen called Scythians, told him tales about warrior women who had in the past (and perhaps still) inhabited the nearby steppes. The Scythians called them "man-killers," while Herodotus called them Amazons after the female fighters of the myths. He later recorded what the Amazonian leaders supposedly told a group of Scythian men who wanted to intermarry with them:

We and the women of your nation could never live together; our ways are too much at variance. We are riders; our business is with the bow and the spear, and we know nothing of women's work; but in your country no woman has anything to do with such things—your women stay at home in their wagons occupied with feminine tasks, and never go out to hunt or for any other purpose. We could not possibly agree [to live like that].[7]

Here, at least in legend, was a society in which women were in charge of their own lives, lands, and destinies. Well into modern times, most historians assumed that such stories were little more than inventions, morality tales used by Greek men to rationalize their highly male-dominated society. Greek women, like the Scythian women Herodotus wrote about, traditionally stayed home, raised the children, and left the tasks of governing and fighting exclusively to their menfolk. By utilizing a total and unflattering gender reversal—namely the savage and unfeminine Amazons— Greek men might show their wives and daughters how improper it was for women to act like men.

In recent years, however, this explanation of the Amazonian tales has steadily given way to the distinct possibility that such warrior women may actually once have roamed the Russian steppes. In the 1950s archaeologists excavating burial mounds of the ancient nomadic inhabitants of the steppes began finding female grave sites containing armor, swords, spears, and arrowheads. An American-Russian excavation

This statue of an Amazon is one of many such depictions of the famous warrior women in ancient Greek art and literature.

13

team discovered more such sites in the mid-1990s. According to one of the team's scholars, Jeannine Davis-Kimball, seven of the forty female graves unearthed contained "iron swords or daggers, bronze arrowheads, and whetstones to sharpen the weapons, suggesting that these seven females were warriors." Moreover,

> the bowed leg bones of one 13- or 14-year-old girl attest a life on horseback, and her array of arms included a dagger and dozens of arrowheads in a quiver made of wood and leather. It seems her amulets were also designed to reinforce her prowess, for she wore a bronze arrowhead in a leather pouch around her neck, and a great boar's tusk . . . lay at her feet. A bent arrowhead was found in the body cavity of another woman, suggesting that she had been killed in battle. . . . Our excavations have shown that some [of these nomadic females of the steppes] held a unique position in society. They seem to have controlled much of the wealth, performed rituals for their families and clan, rode horseback, and possibly hunted . . . steppe antelope, and other small game. In times of stress, where their territory or possessions were threatened, they took to their saddles, bows and arrows ready, to defend their animals, pastures, and clan.[8]

Nomadic tribes like these, in which women played decisive political and military roles, may well have given rise to the legends of the race the Greeks called the Amazons.

Assuming the "Manly" Role

The ancient Greeks had no such hard evidence for the existence of the Amazons, of course. Yet while these particular warrior women long remained the stuff of legend, the Greeks certainly knew about real cases of women who had led their countries in both peace and war. Greek (and later Roman) historians and poets made much ado about an Assyrian queen who had lived in the ninth century B.C. (At the time, Assyria, centered in what is now Iraq, was the dominant empire of the Near East.) When her husband, King Shamshi-Adad V, died, Queen Sammuramat single-handedly ruled Assyria for some five years while waiting for her son to come of age and assume the throne. Little is known about her reign, other than that she was apparently a forceful and efficient ruler. The classical Greeks called her Semiramis and told of her many miraculous and scandalous exploits, some of which probably had no basis in fact. The story that she had a different lover every night

14

and put each to death the next morning, for instance, smacks of fable. On the other hand, some of the impressive engineering feats the Greeks attributed to her may have been exaggerated memories of real projects she initiated. According to Herodotus, for example, she "was responsible for certain remarkable embankments in the plain outside the city [Nineveh, one of Assyria's capitals], built to control the river [the Tigris] which until then used to flood the whole countryside."[9] Semiramis's reputation as a strong woman leader endured into modern times. The eighteenth-century French writer Voltaire wrote a popular play about her in 1748, and the great Italian composer Rossini subsequently turned that play into an opera in 1823 titled *Semiramide*.

The classical Greeks and Romans were even more impressed or disturbed (or both) by the exploits of powerful women who lived in their own times and whose deeds were well documented. Herodotus and others told about Tomyris, a warrior queen who ruled a nomadic tribe on the plains east of the Caspian Sea in the 500s B.C. When Cyrus, the king of Persia (the nation that had by then largely incorporated most of the lands of the defunct Assyrian Empire), tried to invade Tomyris's territory, she attacked, defeated, and killed him in a battle that Herodotus claimed was "more violent than any other fought between foreign [non-Greek] nations."[10]

The "Pestilence of a Woman"

Another warrior woman who led her nation in battle not long after Tomyris was herself a Greek. In the early 400s B.C., Artemisia was the queen of Caria, a Greek territory in what is now southwestern Turkey. The Persians had recently incorporated the area into their growing empire, so they enlisted Artemisia's military aid when they invaded mainland Greece in 480. She showed up in full battle armor, along with five warships and some land troops. During the big Persian-Greek showdown, the sea battle of Salamis (which the Persians soundly lost), she fought so effectively that the Persian king is said to have remarked, "My men have become women, my women men."[11]

The most famous Greek warrior woman, and indeed probably the most famous woman leader of all times, also fought in a great naval battle. Cleopatra, queen of Egypt, stood resolutely on the deck of her war galley in the waters off Actium (in western Greece) in 31 B.C. as she and her lover/ally, Rome's Marcus Antonius (Mark Antony), came to death grips with another powerful Roman, Octavian. The lovers ended up losing the battle and escaping to Egypt, where Octavian eventually came after them.

Cleopatra and her lover, Antony, enjoy the adulation of her subjects. Antony was condemned by many of his fellow Romans for choosing her above his homeland. Some claimed she had bewitched him.

When Cleopatra died soon afterward, she was already a legendary figure; for she had proven herself an intelligent and capable national leader in what a noted historian calls "essentially a man's world." [12] In one of his propaganda speeches against her, Octavian summed up how the Romans viewed any woman who had the gall to think she could assume the "manly" role of ruling a country:

> We Romans are the rulers of the greatest and best parts of the world, and yet we find ourselves spurned [rejected] and trampled upon by a woman of Egypt. This disgraces our fathers . . . [who] would be cut to the heart if ever they knew that we have been overcome by the pestilence of a woman. [13]

When Women Wore the Pants?

Yet while the Greeks and Romans (along with most other ancient, medieval, and early modern peoples) generally disapproved of strong, "take charge" females like Cleopatra and Semiramis, they could not help being fascinated by them. Because such women were so rare and appeared so daring, as well as threatening to the established order, most people tended to believe that they must possess some special, even mystical, attributes. Thus, the real deeds of the warrior women invariably became colored and clouded by both exaggeration and outright lies and people came to hold them in awe at the same time that they resented them. Historian Antonia Fraser suggests that this weird mixture of awe and fear might derive from a racial memory of a time when women, rather than men, wore the pants, so to speak. "Let us suppose," she writes, that

> there is something deep in the human spirit which finds in the image of the strong and armed woman a figure of awe. If that be so, then the next step is to consider whether such awe springs not so much from the human subconscious as from some real state of society in the remote past. Is it possible that the aggressive goddess, far from being a surprising figure, in terms of the patriarchal [male-dominated] attitudes which have generally prevailed, is actually a reflection of the preceding *matriarchal* age when women as a whole were the dominant sex? Thus the Warrior Queen herself might appear as a kind of vestigial [leftover] relic of that distant epoch: hence her encouraging or terrifying aspect [image] according to the contemporary view taken of women's rightful role in society. It is certainly tempting to regard the chariot-driving Warrior Queen as owing her authority to deep memories of a matriarchal society where women either held the reins of the chariot or gave the men the orders which enabled them to do so.[14]

Were the warrior women who roamed the Russian steppes, whom the Greeks called Amazons, a lingering remnant of a primeval age when matriarchies were the rule? No one knows for sure. But even if such societies were once more common, they were probably neither large-scale nor universal; and they were certainly all extinct long before Cleopatra's day. That left her a lone woman ruler in a thoroughly male-dominated Roman world. The Romans could never under any circumstances allow her to succeed, of course, lest she set an example for other such female upstarts.

Bold Boudicca and Zealous Zenobia

Yet despite Cleopatra's untimely demise, in succeeding centuries a few bold women did follow her example and attempted, like she had, to challenge the manly might of the Roman colossus. One of these was Boudicca (also Boudica or Boadicea), the leader of the Iceni, a Celtic tribe in south-central Britain. Under the formidable Julius Caesar, the Romans had made initial inroads into Britain in the first century B.C. In the A.D. 40s, however, they launched a major invasion and made much of the island into the Roman province of Britannia. As might be expected, this did not sit well with the natives, including the Iceni; however, most found little choice but to cooperate with the vastly superior Roman military.

Things changed when the king of the Iceni died in about the year 60. He was good enough to leave half his kingdom and royal treasury to Nero, then Rome's emperor.[15] But this was not good enough for Britannia's governor, who, according to the Roman historian Tacitus, plundered the dead man's "kingdom and household alike." The king's widow, Boudicca, "was flogged and her daughters raped."[16] This was the last straw for the Iceni. Acknowledging Boudicca as their new queen and war leader, they launched a full-scale rebellion, which tens of thousands of warriors from neighboring tribes eagerly joined. Boudicca led them against the Roman stronghold of Londinium (now London), utterly destroying it, and went on to massacre over seventy thousand Roman settlers. Like Cleopatra and Egypt, however, Boudicca and Britain could not stand up to the fearsome force of a well-equipped and highly trained Roman army, one of which finally confronted and defeated the rebels. "At first," Tacitus wrote, the Roman troops

> stood their ground. Keeping to the defile [narrow gorge] as a natural defense, they launched their javelins accurately at the approaching enemy. Then, in wedge-formation, they burst forward. . . . The cavalry, too, with lances extended, demolished all serious resistance. The remaining Britons fled with difficulty since their ring of wagons blocked the outlets. The Romans did not spare even the women. Baggage animals too, transfixed [run through] with weapons, added to the heaps of dead.[17]

Presumably, Boudicca committed suicide before the Romans could capture her and display her in their victory parade. The location of her tomb, constructed later by her people, remains unknown,

This engraving, like many other later artistic depictions of Boudicca, the bold Celtic princess, shows her riding her chariot.

despite numerous modern monuments scattered across the British countryside, each claiming to mark her final resting place.

Another uppity queen who stood up to Rome was Zenobia of the prosperous city-state of Palmyra, located in the Near Eastern region of Syria. The Palmyran king, Odaenathus, allied himself with the Romans in the mid–third century A.D. Soon afterward, however, he declared his independence and claimed ownership of many of the Near Eastern territories the Romans deemed vital to their empire. When Odaenathus died in 267, his widow, Zenobia, who was even more audacious than he was, invaded and annexed Egypt and other neighboring lands. Politically savvy as well as brave, Zenobia reinforced her formidable persona by claiming descent from the legendary Cleopatra. As Fraser points out:

> She quickly appreciated the self-aggrandizement [enhancement of her image] to be derived from a glamorous historic connection. As Cleopatra used the image of the goddess Isis, the Queen of War, to lend exciting credence to her own dreams of empire, so Zenobia drew Cleopatra's own image to her. She also incidentally associated herself with Semiramis.[18]

The zealous Zenobia managed to hold out against the Romans for over five years—until the emperor Aurelian (reigned 270–275) defeated her and dismantled her short-lived empire. She suffered the indignity of marching in chains in Aurelian's victory parade; but she had the last laugh, for he died soon afterward and she went on to make a new life for herself in Italy. There, near the capital, Zenobia lived out the rest of her days in a luxurious villa, granted to her partly out of respect for her beauty, intelligence, and many talents, which rivaled those of the most educated Roman men. Edward Gibbon called her an "accomplished woman" who was

> perhaps the only female whose superior genius broke through the servile indolence imposed on her sex by the [male-dominated] climate and manners of Asia. She . . . was esteemed the most lovely as well as the most heroic of her sex. . . . Her manly understanding was strengthened and adorned by study. She was not ignorant of the Latin tongue, but possessed in equal perfection the Greek, Syriac, and the Egyptian languages.[19]

"The Grand Countess"

Gibbon's admiration for warrior queens was not confined to ancient women like Zenobia. "Modern Europe," he wrote, "has produced several illustrious women who have sustained with glory the weight of empire; nor is our own age destitute of such distinguished characters."[20] Indeed, during the many centuries that elapsed between the disintegration of Greco-Roman civilization (500s–600s) and Gibbon's time (1700s), perhaps a dozen or more strong and/or controversial women ruled various European kingdoms or domains. This was not a large number considering the thousands of men who held great power or high governmental positions in the same period. (The number excludes such figures as France's Joan of Arc and England's Mother Ross; although these and other courageous women led or fought alongside men in wartime, they did not rule nations, or as Gibbon phrased it, "sustain the weight of empire.")

In fact, most of the strong, capable, and ambitious women of the medieval and early modern centuries, like their ancient sisters, found their lives and fortunes largely shaped by ruthless competition with strong and ambitious men. Take the case of Matilda, countess of Tuscany (in central Italy). Later known as "the Grand Countess," she used up much of her lifetime and substantial energies opposing one dominating man after another. Her father, Boniface, who ruled over the huge Italian domains of the powerful House of Canossa, was assassinated in 1052; when both her mother and her husband died in 1076, she became the sole heir of the Canossan realm.

Almost immediately, Matilda was caught in the middle of a vehement dispute between two of the most powerful men of the day. Pope Gregory VII believed that only he and other popes should be allowed to invest (confer offices and titles on) bishops and other clergymen. Germany's emperor, Henry IV, insisted on retaining the time-honored custom of secular rulers investing the clergy. Matilda threw her considerable wealth and influence behind the pope, who proceeded to excommunicate Henry (exclude him from church rites and community), and at first this double whammy seemed to do the trick. In January 1077 Henry journeyed to Matilda's castle at Canossa and there, in the freezing winter cold (according to Gregory's report to Henry's German lords),

> presented himself at the gate of the castle, barefoot and clad only in wretched woolen garments, beseeching us with fears to grant him absolution and forgiveness. This he continued to do for three days, while all those around us were moved to compassion at his plight. . . . At length we removed the excommunication from him, and received him again into the bosom of Holy Mother Church.[21]

Zenobia gazes for the last time on her beloved native city of Palmyra.

Despite this submission to the pope's will, Henry later renewed the dispute and turned his soldiers loose on Matilda to punish her for supporting his opponent. Several times she personally led her own troops against those of the German emperor and his Italian allies. Her most stunning triumph was a battle fought near the Tuscan town of Sorbara in 1084, where her soldiers loudly chanted the war cry, "For St. Peter and Matilda!" Not until after Henry died in 1106 and she concluded a peace treaty with his son, Henry V, in 1110 did Matilda begin to enjoy a serene and secure life. Still, the conflict between the papacy and German monarchs continued after her death in July

1115, for in her will she gave some of her lands to the popes and some to Henry V, and each claimed rights over the whole lot.

Their Policies Shaped by Faith

Religious faith and strife turned out to be recurring themes in the lives and reigns of many of the women European rulers who succeeded Matilda. Isabella was crowned queen of the Spanish kingdom of Castile in 1474. Like her husband, Ferdinand, heir to the throne of Aragon (another Spanish kingdom), Isabella was a staunch Catholic. Her religious zeal shaped many of her policies. These included her support of the Spanish Inquisition, a kind of kangaroo court organized by the church to root out and punish nonbelievers, and her persecution of Spanish Jews. In a similar vein, Queen Elizabeth I concluded the so-called Elizabethan Settlement for the Church of England shortly after ascending the English throne in 1558. Conflict between Catholics and Protestants had been fierce ever since her father, Henry VIII, had broken with the papacy in 1533. Elizabeth's half sister, Mary I (reigned 1553–1558), had briefly restored papal authority in England; but Elizabeth, who was herself a Protestant, once more excluded that authority. Elizabeth also later sent English troops to support the Protestant side in Protestant-Catholic conflicts in France and Holland.

One prominent European queen went so far as to give up her throne for her religious beliefs. In 1632, twenty-nine years after Elizabeth's death, King Gustavus Adolphus, of the Protestant country of Sweden, was killed in battle and his six-year-old daughter, Christina, became queen. Given an excellent education, this brilliant, strong-willed young woman took full control of the country at age eighteen (1644). An effective politician, she was a prime mover in the negotiations that led to the treaty ending the Thirty Years' War, the conflict that had claimed her father's life. Christina displayed a passion for culture and learning, especially theology and philosophy, and spoke seven languages;[22] and during her reign Sweden benefited from both its first newspaper and a bill providing for the building of schools nationwide.

In 1654, at the height of her power and vigor, however, Christina suddenly abdicated her throne. She had secretly converted to Catholicism, a faith forbidden in Sweden. Leaving her cousin, Charles Gustavus, as the nation's new monarch, she traveled to Rome, where the pope welcomed the famous new convert. Christina remained a patron of the arts and enjoyed close friendships with four successive popes until her death in 1689. (Several Christian European rulers remained confused and put off by her abdication, however; considering the historical struggles women had waged to maintain powerful positions in a man's world, her voluntary exile must have made Cleopatra, Boudicca, and Matilda turn over in their graves.)

Man's Better Half

Most of the women leaders of nations who followed Christina were much more reluctant to give up their powerful positions. Some, like Catherine II and Victoria, did so only when death intervened. Catherine, whom one famous writer called "the Semiramis of the north," ruled Russia with a strong hand for thirty-four years (1762–1796); and Victoria reigned over the British for sixty-four years (1837–1901), imparting her name to one of England's greatest ages. The few notable women leaders who emerged in the twentieth century served democracies, so the lengths of their "reigns," so to speak, were therefore limited by legal term limits or other constitutional procedures. An exception was Indira Gandhi, who served intermittently as India's prime minister from 1966 to 1984, and who was assassinated. The other recent famous and influential women prime ministers, Israel's Golda Meir (beginning in 1969), Britain's Margaret Thatcher (be-

England's stalwart Queen Elizabeth I was sometimes referred to as the "Virgin Queen."

ginning in 1979), and Pakistan's Benazir Bhutto (beginning in 1988), all served their nations and then returned to private life.

None of these modern women were alike in temperament or background, or faced the same political and social problems. Like national leaders of the past, both male and female, each brought her own unique skills, values, philosophies, and experiences to the job and left her own special mark on the historical record. Yet women leaders in all ages had two qualities in common. First, almost all presided over the ravages of war at least once during their watches (although Elizabeth, Catherine, Victoria, Meir, Thatcher, and others in recent times did not actually lead their troops into battle as Artemesia, Boudicca, and Matilda did).

In addition to the image of the warrior woman, these leaders shared the equally powerful maternal image. Despite whether she produced children of her own, each was identified by her people, to one degree or another, as their "national mother," the nurturer and protectress of their property, values, and way of life. By exploiting this image, these leaders were often able to turn their gender's usual social and political disadvantage into a decided advantage. "Motherhood is, after all, the one role which is totally closed to men," Fraser points out.

> Soon the "Mother of her Country" begins to be seen in a supernatural rather than an unnatural light. . . . The supernatural aura of the Warrior Queen has the . . . effect of sanctifying the nation's struggle in its own eyes: and all through history it is always good for morale to be fighting a holy war.[23]

Christina, queen of Sweden in the mid-1600s, abdicated her throne after secretly converting to Catholicism. She later befriended four successive popes.

Countries, like people, need and identify with both mothers *and* fathers, of course. The goal of queens and women politicians has never been to replace all the male leaders with females, as the Amazons were said to have done. Rather, the lives and struggles of such women should be seen as part of a slow but steady progression toward political parity and a world of true equal opportunity. The outspoken Lady Astor, who in 1919 became the first woman member of the British Parliament, herself a national leader of sorts, left behind what could be viewed in a sense as a creed for woman leaders through the ages:

> Now, why are we in politics? . . . I believe that one of the reasons why civilization has failed so lamentably is that it has had a one-sided government. Don't let us make the mistake of ever allowing that to happen again. I can conceive of nothing worse than a man-governed world except a woman-governed world—but I can see the combination of the two going forward and making civilization more worthy. . . . We [women] must go on being his [man's] guide, his mother, and his better half. But we must prove to him that we are a necessary half not only in private but [also] in political life.[24]

CHAPTER 2

Cleopatra:
A Woman for All Ages

Cleopatra VII, queen of Egypt, became a legend not only in her own time, the turbulent first century B.C., but for all time. Her fame rests mainly on her relationships, both political and intimate, with two of the most powerful men of her world—the Roman statesmen Julius Caesar and Mark Antony. But her unique wit, charm, and boldness, along with her fabulously grand and extravagant lifestyle, also contributed to her larger-than-life persona. Later writings, historical accounts and fictional tales alike, tended to stress her sensational aspects and deeds. In so doing they inevitably exaggerated and distorted many of the facts (propaganda and fable are often more colorful, dramatic, and romantic than truth, after all).

Thus were born the many stereotypes and half-truths about her—that, for instance, she was a scheming enchantress who used her spells to lure great men to their doom. Largely blaming her for Antony's fall from grace, the Greek historian and moralist Plutarch (who lived about a century later) wrote:

> The love for Cleopatra which now entered his life came as the final and crowning mischief which could befall him. It excited to the point of madness many passions which had hitherto [before] lain concealed, or at least dormant, and it stifled or corrupted all those redeeming qualities in him which were still capable of resisting temptation. . . . Cleopatra . . . had already seen for herself the power of her beauty to enchant Julius Caesar . . . and she expected to conquer Antony even more easily. . . . She therefore provided herself with as lavish a supply of gifts, money, and ornaments as her exalted position . . . made it appropriate to take, but she relied above all upon her physical presence and the spell and enchantment which it could create.[25]

Thanks to exaggerated, judgmental tracts like this one and many others even more fanciful and derogatory, the Egyptian queen's

25

highly romantic legend continued to grow. Eventually her deeds became the subject of numerous poems, plays, books, and movies, most of which did not (and often could not) separate fact from fiction.

Modern historians have fortunately managed, to some degree, to separate the real from the mythical Cleopatra. The woman who emerges from their studies is an intelligent, resourceful, and able ruler, in every way the equal of the male statesmen of her day. Was she crafty, manipulative, and grandly ambitious? Yes. But then, so were the famous men with whom she competed. She was also more politically astute, educated, talented, generous, loyal, and worldly than all but two or three of them. All the innuendoes and romantic hype aside, it is the fact that she dared to vie with them for power and thereby threatened to topple their staunchly male-dominated social order that made her a larger-than-life woman for all ages.

The Piper Pays Rome

Born in 69 B.C., Cleopatra was the daughter of Egypt's ruler, Ptolemy XII, popularly known as Auletes, or "the Piper," because of his skill as a flute player. The Ptolemaic dynasty, or family line, had been established in the early third century B.C. When the famous Greek conqueror Alexander the Great died unexpectedly in 323 B.C., his

This carving, adorning the Egyptian temple at Dendera, shows Cleopatra wearing the mystic crown of Isis, a deity then popular throughout the Mediterranean world.

leading generals almost immediately began fighting for possession of his huge empire, which included the entire Near East. The bloody power struggle lasted several decades, and finally three major Greek kingdoms (referred to as the Hellenistic realms[26]) emerged. One of Alexander's heirs, Ptolemy, took charge of the kingdom consisting mainly of Egypt, and it was Ptolemy's royal line that later produced the legendary Cleopatra. The Ptolemies ruled Egypt as it had always been ruled, as an absolute monarchy. Most of the Ptolemies, including Auletes, Cleopatra's father, were mediocre and unsympathetic leaders who refused even to bother learning the local language. The result was a cultural barrier between the Egyptian masses and the unpopular royal court, where Greek language and ways remained supreme.

By the time Cleopatra was born, Egypt, though rich in gold and grain, was a third-rate power in a Mediterranean world dominated completely by Roman might. Noted scholar Naphtali Lewis explains:

> As Roman power spread eastward in the second century B.C., it came into conflict with one Hellenistic kingdom, then another; but Egypt . . . was given protection by Rome on occasions when the need arose. Protection evolved . . . into protectorate [a state controlled by a superior power]. Long before the last Cleopatra ascended the throne of her ancestors, Egypt, though . . . still independent, had become in reality a client [dependent] state of all-powerful Rome.[27]

The immediate chain of events leading to Cleopatra's rise as the lone woman ruler in this decidedly male-dominated Roman world began in 59 B.C., when she was ten. Her father, whose mismanagement of Egypt's finances and other blunders had brought the Egyptians to the brink of rebellion, sought to strengthen his position, both at home and abroad. He asked some of the strongest, richest, and most influential Romans of the day, including Julius Caesar, to declare him a "friend and ally" of Rome. This lofty title, Auletes hoped, would make him more feared in Egypt. Caesar and the others agreed, but demanded large bribes in return, which further drained Auletes' already dwindling treasury.

The plan did not work, however, as conditions in Egypt continued to worsen and Auletes' authority there steadily diminished; and in 57 B.C. he traveled to Rome in an attempt to gather more foreign support. In his absence his daughter (and Cleopatra's sister), Cleopatra Tryphainia, seized the Egyptian throne. When she was promptly murdered by Auletes' few remaining supporters, another daughter, Berenice, grabbed power for herself. For a hefty price, a Roman nobleman helped Auletes regain his throne. But all of his efforts eventually came to nothing. He died, hated by nearly everyone and miserable, in 51 B.C. In his will, he stipulated that

Cleopatra, now age eighteen, and her ten-year-old brother, Ptolemy XIII, would jointly rule the country.

The Political Reality of the Day

Cleopatra's reign was at first troubled by tensions and rivalries. Her brother's regent (adult adviser and protector), Pothinus, the most powerful figure in the Egyptian court, resented her and wanted to see the boy become sole ruler. Taking every opportunity to discredit Cleopatra, Pothinus blamed her for the country's continuing economic problems. She became so unpopular at court that in September 49 B.C. she was forced to flee the capital, Alexandria, and go into hiding in the desert.

Cleopatra's exile was short-lived, however. Fortunately for her, the Roman state was undergoing major power realignments, which came to a head in a bloody civil war. The formidable generals Julius Caesar and Gnaeus Pompey faced off, and Cleopatra reasoned that one or both of these men would need and seek Egyptian grain and money to support his troops. Unlike Ptolemy, Pothinus, and her other adversaries at the court, who hated and staunchly resisted Roman influence, she recognized the political reality of the day. Making and exploiting alliances with strong Roman men was the logical way for any minor ruler, especially a female one, to get ahead.

Cleopatra's chance to form such an alliance came sooner than even she expected. In 48 B.C. Caesar decisively defeated Pompey at Pharsalus, in Greece, and Pompey turned to Egypt's leaders for protection and support. In his *Commentary on the Civil Wars*, Caesar recorded:

> It happened that the boy-king Ptolemy was at Pelusium [in northern Egypt] with a large army. He was at [odds] with his sister Cleopatra, whom he had driven from the throne a few months earlier. . . . Pompey sent [messengers] to Ptolemy asking him . . . to receive him into Alexandria and to use his power to protect him in his misfortune.[28]

When Caesar arrived in Egypt, in pursuit of Pompey, he found that Ptolemy and Pothinus had ordered Pompey's murder. "It may be," Caesar later wrote,

> that they were really afraid that Pompey might tamper with the loyalty of the royal army and occupy Alexandria. . . . Or it may be that they regarded his prospects [in the war] as hopeless and acted according to the common rule by which a man's friends become his enemies in adversity.[29]

Whatever their motives, Ptolemy and Pothinus expected Caesar to be pleased when they presented him with Pompey's severed head. Far from pleased, Caesar was actually outraged to see such savage treatment of a great Roman leader. Moreover, he suddenly and firmly demanded that the Egyptians pay him a large sum, supposedly some of Auletes' still outstanding debts.

Captivated by the Queen

Meanwhile, seeing her chance to take Caesar's side against her enemies, Cleopatra acted boldly. According to Plutarch:

> Taking only one of her friends with her, (Apollodorus the Sicilian), [she] embarked in a small boat and landed at the palace when it was already getting dark. Since there seemed to be no other way of getting in, she stretched herself out at full length inside a sleeping bag, and Apollodorus, after tying up the bag, carried it indoors to Caesar. This little trick of Cleopatra's, which showed her provocative impudence, is said to have been the first thing about her which captivated Caesar.[30]

This conceptual sketch for a production of Shakespeare's Antony and Cleopatra *emphasizes her supposed exotic beauty. Surprisingly, likenesses of her on ancient coins suggest she was not so physically attractive.*

Caesar was so captivated by the Egyptian queen that the two quickly became lovers, despite the age difference: He was fifty-two, she was only twenty-one. Proceeding to back Cleopatra in the local power struggle, Caesar demanded that she and Ptolemy marry and rule jointly as Auletes had intended. Ptolemy and Pothinus unwisely chose to defy and fight Caesar, and both soon paid for the mistake with their lives.

An eminently practical man, Caesar realized that Cleopatra, as his lover and confidant, would make him and Rome a valuable ally. He reinstalled her on the Egyptian throne with great pomp and ceremony. He also tried to please the Egyptians by having Cleopatra, according to local custom, marry her surviving brother, twelve-year-old Ptolemy XIV. Since this young man had no powerful regent like Pothinus, Cleopatra was now, in effect, sole ruler of Egypt.

Caesar's Untimely Demise

Caesar lingered for some months in Egypt, during which time Cleopatra took him on a pleasure cruise up the Nile.[31] He departed in 47 B.C., leaving her with child, but about a year later he summoned her and the baby boy to Rome to witness the parades celebrating his victories in the civil war. According to the second-century Roman historian Suetonius, Caesar heaped "high titles and rich presents" on her. "He even allowed her to call the son whom she had borne him by his own name." Thus, the child became widely known as Caesarion, although his Egyptian title was Ptolemy XV. "The boy closely resembled Caesar," Suetonius added, "in features as well as in gait."[32]

Caesar did not live long enough to get to know his son. On March 15, 44 B.C., a group of Roman senators, angry that Caesar had recently declared himself dictator for life, stabbed him to death in the Senate House. His close friend and supporter, the powerful general Mark Antony, managed to discredit the conspirators, most of whom fled Italy for Greece. With her famous benefactor and protector dead, Cleopatra thought it prudent to take Caesarion back to Egypt, and they reached Alexandria in July.

Gaius Julius Caesar (pictured), a shrewd politician and one of the greatest military strategists in history, fathered Cleopatra's first child, Caesarion.

The Second Triumvirate

During the two years following Caesar's assassination, three ambitious men stepped into the power vacuum he had left. Antony,

Octavian (Caesar's eighteen-year-old adopted son), and Lepidus (a popular general) formed an alliance known as the Second Triumvirate, aiming to "restore order" by establishing a three-man dictatorship. They killed many of their political opponents in a reign of terror while simultaneously preparing to fight the leaders of the conspiracy against Caesar, who were raising their own troops in Greece.

Cleopatra knew that the best course for her was to back the party most likely to win the ensuing conflict. But at the time it was impossible to know who the victor would be. She took the safe course and claimed she was unable to help either side, citing as an excuse ongoing bouts of pestilence and famine in her land. She watched with interest as the triumvirs defeated the conspirators in Greece in 42 B.C. and then greedily proceeded to divide up the Roman world among themselves. Antony got the wealthiest and most populous part—the East, giving him control of the Roman provinces in Greece and the Near East and influence over weak independent eastern kingdoms like Egypt.

This turn of events inevitably brought Antony and Cleopatra into close contact.[33] In need of Egyptian money and grain, in the late summer of 41 B.C. he summoned her to his headquarters at Tarsus, in southern Asia Minor (what is now Turkey), and there she made one of history's most memorable entrances. "She came sailing up the river Cydnus," Plutarch wrote,

> in a barge with a stern of gold, its purple sails billowing in the wind, while her rowers caressed the water with oars of silver which dipped in time to the music of the flute, accompanied by pipes and lutes. Cleopatra herself reclined beneath a canopy of gold cloth, dressed as Venus [goddess of love] . . . while on either side . . . stood boys costumed as Cupids, who cooled her with fans.[34]

Antony—Her "Sexual Captive"?

Antony was apparently even more captivated by Cleopatra than Caesar had been. Ancient historians made much of the ensuing love affair between Antony and the Egyptian queen and blamed her for his subsequent turn against his own country and steady slide into political and moral oblivion. These accounts usually pictured her as a "wicked creature" who had "bewitched" him, made him her "sexual captive," and "deprived him of his wits." In retrospect, it is clear that such distortions, which sullied Cleopatra's name for centuries to come, were tainted by strong Roman biases against both foreigners and any woman who dared to intrude in the "manly" game of politics. On the one hand, however, Antony was an alcoholic, an inept administrator, and a headstrong adventurer given to making bad decisions; on the other, he and Cleopatra were mature and ambitious adults who saw the chance to use each other to their own ends and to enjoy themselves at the same time. In short, the blame for Antony's mistakes lies ultimately with Antony.

They Could Not Erase Her Memory

Perhaps what drew Antony to Cleopatra was the fact that she, a foreign woman, had so many of the personal leadership qualities that he, a Roman man, sorely lacked. During much of the time that they were allied, she administered Egypt alone; evidence suggests that she was a caring, capable, and efficient ruler who managed the economy well and treated her people justly. During her reign, in glaring contrast to those of her predecessors, there were no rebellions and tax collection proceeded normally. She improved and expanded agriculture,

Like Caesar, Mark Antony, pictured in this bust, found Cleopatra captivating. Eventually, Antony, unlike Caesar, betrayed Rome for her.

producing large surpluses of grain and other foodstuffs, thus eliminating food shortages and lowering food prices. In addition, she took the time to become fluent in the local language and used it, along with Greek, at court, and she went to great lengths to observe Egyptian religious rites. These efforts, largely neglected by the earlier Ptolemies, won her the support of many Egyptians who had long distrusted the foreign dynasty.

Unfortunately for Cleopatra and Egypt, her talents as a ruler could not keep her and her country from being engulfed in the dangerous currents of Rome's latest power struggle. The Second Triumvirate fell to pieces as Antony, commanding the East, and Octavian, in charge of the West, squared off in a new civil war.[35] Cleopatra backed Antony, partly out of loyalty (by this time they had children together) and also in Egypt's national interest (if Antony won, the country might regain much of its former greatness). To everyone's surprise, the war's outcome was decided largely by a single battle, fought at sea near the Greek town of Actium on September 2, 31 B.C. Thanks to Octavian's brilliant military strategist, Marcus Agrippa, Antony and Cleopatra suffered a major defeat, although the lovers managed to break free with some of their ships and escape to Egypt. There, they evidently planned to use Cleopatra's treasure to build a new fleet and launch a fresh offensive.

But the lovers soon realized that their cause was lost. Most of Antony's troops deserted him, and none of Cleopatra's neighbors were willing to risk incurring Octavian's wrath by sending troops,

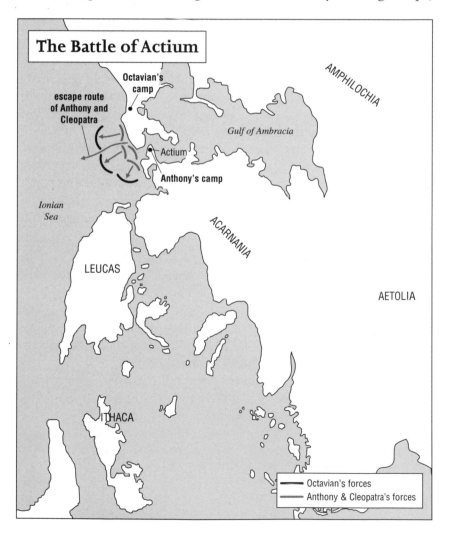

The Battle of Actium

Octavian's camp

escape route of Anthony and Cleopatra

AMPHILOCHIA

Gulf of Ambracia

Actium

Anthony's camp

Ionian Sea

ACARNANIA

LEUCAS

AETOLIA

ITHACA

Octavian's forces
Anthony & Cleopatra's forces

supplies, or other support. Alone in Alexandria, their dreams of a new Mediterranean world order dashed, Antony and Cleopatra waited for the inevitable showdown with Octavian, who finally advanced on the city in July 30 B.C. Humiliated and distraught over his losses and mistakenly informed that his lover was dead, Antony committed suicide. Soon afterward Octavian took Cleopatra into custody. Octavian's plans for the "treacherous creature" who had caused Rome so much trouble included marching her in chains through the streets of Rome to show what would happen to women who did not know their place in the Roman world. She robbed him of that satisfaction, however, by taking her own life.

In her thirty-nine years, twenty-one of them as Egypt's queen, Cleopatra had demonstrated as much intelligence, political skills, and sheer courage and audacity as the powerful male leaders with whom she had dealt. In the end, the male-dominated system devoured her; but it could not erase the memory of her extraordinary personality and deeds, nor could it destroy the future vision she stood for and dreamed of—a world in which men and women might meet on an even playing field. In a sense, then, as historian Peter Green says, "Cleopatra achieved her dying wish." Only Alexander the Great, her renowned Greek predecessor, Green suggests, "eclipsed the mesmeric [hypnotic] fascination that she exercised down the centuries, and still exercises, upon the European imagination: the perennial symbol of what, had Actium gone the other way, might have been a profoundly different world."[36] Thus is the end of her story, like its beginning, wrapped in the stuff of legend.

CHAPTER 3

Isabella:
"The Traveling Queen"

Isabella I, queen of the Spanish kingdom of Castile, stood at a crucial crossroads in European history. First, she and her husband, Ferdinand II, leader of another Spanish domain, Aragon, were largely responsible for unifying Spain into one of Europe's most powerful and influential nations. At the time of Isabella's birth, in the mid–fifteenth century, the Iberian peninsula was composed of five major regions. On the western coast lay the large Christian kingdom of Portugal. Farther east, occupying the central portion of the peninsula, was another Christian kingdom, Castile, the largest of the five regions. Two more Christian lands—tiny Navarre and the larger Aragon—made up the peninsula's northeastern section. And finally there was Granada, in the far south, the last stronghold of the Moors, the Muslim group that had controlled much of the peninsula in prior centuries. By combining their rule of Castile and Aragon, and conquering Granada and Navarre, the "Catholic Kings," as Isabella and Ferdinand became known, made Spain a single, mighty nation.

The other great accomplishment that Isabella presented to posterity was her sponsorship of the renowned Italian explorer Christopher Columbus. Her relentless drive to seek new resources for her country eventually led her to share Columbus's vision of sailing westward to the "Indies." As a result, Spain acquired valuable overseas territories. Moreover, Columbus's voyages helped to inspire a burgeoning age of world exploration; even after Spain's power and influence faded in subsequent centuries, its legacy endured in the form of new and expansive global trade routes and settlements.

Because these important positive achievements have loomed large in the Western consciousness over the centuries, they have tended to overshadow Isabella's less admirable acts. She was undoubtedly a strong-willed, talented, and tireless ruler, but she was also religiously intolerant and horribly persecuted those of her

Spain (c. 1450)

subjects who did not accept her Christian beliefs. At the time, most people in Spain and other parts of Europe agreed with Isabella's rigid religious stance and praised her for it. An Italian notable wrote that

> unless all the people of Spain, men and women, rich and poor, have combined to tell lies in her praise, there has not been in our time in the whole world a brighter example of true goodness, greatness of spirit, wisdom, religion, honor, courtesy, liberality, and every virtue, in short, than this Queen Isabella.[37]

From a modern vantage, Isabella, who hounded and killed Muslims and Jews, was not the saint described in this tract. Historians point out that she was, with all her virtues and faults, a product of the intellectual and moral climate of her time, and her mistakes must be judged in that context. "In truth," comments Nancy Rubin, one of her recent biographers, "Isabella was neither saint nor sinner. Ultimately her monumental accomplishments were simply rooted in human fallibility."[38]

Isabella's Childhood

Isabella was born on April 22, 1451, the daughter of King Juan (John) II of Castile and Isabella, a Portuguese noblewoman. In 1454, when young princess Isabella was barely three, her father died and Enrique (Henry) IV, Juan's son from a previous marriage, inherited Castile's throne. Castilian custom demanded that a widowed queen and her children leave the royal court after a monarch's death. Enrique immediately sent Isabella of Portugal and her daughter to live in a remote Castilian castle, where they spent the next several years.

For a long time, no one expected that the young Isabella would end up ruling the kingdom. Thus, she received the minimal education that was common for young women from good families. She was exposed, Rubin writes,

Isabella, queen of Castile. Willful and obstinate, she set her sights on marrying Ferdinand, heir to the throne of Aragon.

> to conventional "women's books" such as Louis de Leon's *The Perfect Wife . . .* and Juan Ruiz's *The Book of Good Love,* allegorical tales that . . . offered examples of virtuous women. Like most high-born children, Isabella also read heroic tales of chivalry, among them the tales of King Arthur. . . . Although Isabella's brothers were thoroughly schooled in the classics, the princess was taught "cultivation of the womanly virtues"—reading and writing . . . prayers, the Bible, embroidery, needlepoint, and gilded painting.[39]

Despite her limited schooling, Isabella proved to be politically astute at a very young age. When she reached her midteens, she negotiated with King Enrique to have him name her as heir to the Castilian throne and to refrain from forcing her to marry against her wishes. Apparently she had already made up her mind whom she wanted to wed, namely her distant cousin Ferdinand of

Aragon. Although she had not yet met him, she had heard, through relatives and friends, that he was handsome, charming, intelligent, and had the makings of a fine ruler. More importantly, he was heir to Aragon's throne. Even at this early date, Isabella envisioned the tremendous potential of unifying the two realms into a greater Spain.

With these grand and romantic plans in mind, Isabella was understandably upset when Enrique suddenly reneged on their agreement and demanded that she marry someone else. Undaunted, however, she boldly sent a secret marriage agreement to Ferdinand's father, King Juan II of Aragon, who was delighted by the prospect of his son marrying her. Early in October 1469, Ferdinand, accompanied by a small band of Aragonese nobles, rode overland to the Castilian town of Valladolid. There, on October 14, at night and by torchlight, a fittingly romantic setting for the idealistic young couple, Isabella, then eighteen, and Ferdinand, seventeen, first laid eyes on each other. According to a contemporary Spanish chronicler, "In that meeting, the presence of the Archbishop [who was to conduct the marriage] restrained the amorous impulses of the lovers, whose strong hearts [were] filled with the joy and delight of matrimony." [40] The two were married the next day. Against considerable odds, their union would turn out to be a long, happy, and fruitful one.

The New Queen and Her Consort

Not surprisingly, Enrique was furious when he learned of her secret marriage. He called the union "unauthorized," and therefore invalid, and attempted to destroy it. But he was unsuccessful. The Castilian noble houses were divided over who should be heir to the throne and public disorder and civil strife erupted in many parts of the kingdom. During this troubled time Isabella rode from one town to another, gaining the support of various nobles, which earned her the nickname of "the Traveling Queen." Sick of Enrique's arrogance and mismanagement of the realm, an increasing number of powerful lords took her side.

All-out civil war was averted, however, when Enrique died unexpectedly in December 1474. On hearing the news, Isabella, who was then in Segovia in north-central Castile, immediately proclaimed herself queen. The Cortes, a parliament made up of representatives from the major towns, and many noble houses swiftly swore allegiance to her, solidifying her position. According to the unique marriage agreement between Isabella and Ferdinand, they were to rule the two kingdoms jointly, but each would retain ultimate sovereignty in his or her own kingdom. Thus, Ferdinand could wield considerable power in Castile; but on paper Isabella was its monarch and he was merely her consort. The agreement further stipulated that if the royal couple produced a male heir the boy would, when they died, become king of a united Spain.

Isabella and Ferdinand found their rule immediately and severely tested. In 1475, trying to topple Isabella from her throne, King Alfonso V of Portugal invaded Castile with some twenty thousand troops. The queen went on the road again, mustering support and managing to raise thousands of loyal troops of her own. In the war's first major engagement, however, her troops failed to take an enemy town and retreated. In a remarkable speech, excerpted here, Isabella both reprimanded her troops for their failure and challenged them to do better:

> I would wish to pursue uncertain danger rather than certain shame. . . . There must first be a battle in order to be a victory. . . . I find myself in my palace, with angry heart and closed teeth and clenched fists. . . . Of my fury, being a woman, and of your patience, being men, I marvel. . . . The ill-effect on your service on the kingdom, on foreign opinion and on the honor of our honors hurts. I bare my soul, because it is not within myself, suffering in spirit, that I can alleviate the pain, nor drive it out; for it is certain that the best rest for the afflicted is to vent their ills.[41]

Isabella and Ferdinand managed to overcome the setback. They borrowed money from the clergy and Ferdinand used it to reorganize the army, which decisively defeated Alfonso's forces in 1476. Three important events then followed in rapid succession, each proving fortunate for the royal couple. In 1478 Isabella gave birth to a son, Prince Juan; in January 1479 Aragon's Juan II died, allowing Ferdinand to assume the throne; and in October 1479 Portugal's Alfonso signed a treaty officially ending the war he had begun five years before.

A Land Transformed

Her rule now secure, Isabella, with her husband's help, proceeded to initiate a number of radical reforms that quickly transformed Castile into what was in effect a new country. The *Santa Hermandad,* a national police force composed of common people from each town, patrolled the roads and countryside, rooting out bandits and other criminals who had become alarmingly more numerous in recent decades. A well-trained standing army of some two thousand troops supported the police. Justice was swift and often brutal: Suspects were summarily tried and punished right where they were captured, and penalties included hacking off hands or feet for offenses as mild as petty thievery. Needless to say, the crime rate fell almost overnight.

Isabella also sought to increase her control of the Castilian nobles, whose great wealth, influence, and armed castles still posed a potential threat to her or any monarch. At her order, thousands of castles were destroyed, thereby crippling the aristocracy's ability to wage war.[42] In addition, many of the nobles' traditional ceremonies were abolished and the wealthy had to forfeit large sums of money and valuables to the crown. In conjunction with far-reaching economic reforms, these measures greatly enhanced the authority of the realm's central, royal government.[43]

While overseeing these secular reforms, Isabella instituted some rather drastic religious policies. Although intended to strengthen the Spanish people and the country as a whole, these policies caused

Many of Isabella's secular policies were progressive, while her religious reforms were mostly regressive, even cruel.

much injustice and misery. First, Isabella and Ferdinand received permission from the pope in Rome to set up an inquisition, a church tribunal charged with finding and eliminating heretics, in Spain. Isabella's closest church advisers convinced her that the new Spain she and her husband were building could not be strong and endure unless it achieved "spiritual and racial" unity. This meant essentially that all those who wavered in the slightest from devout Catholicism must convert, leave, or die. Ignoring the rules of evidence and utilizing horrendous tortures and executions, the Spanish Inquisition killed some two thousand people and maimed and terrorized many thousands more between the late 1470s and late 1490s.

Spanish Jews and Muslims suffered most from the religious crusade. In March 1492 Isabella and Ferdinand issued an edict ordering all Jews either to convert to Christianity or leave Spain. "In the time of six months allowed by the edict," a contemporary Spanish historian recorded, the Jews

> sold and sold cheaply what they could of their estates. . . . The Christians got their very rich houses and heirlooms for little money. . . . Some [Jews] sorrowfully converted and stayed, but very few. . . . When those who went to embark [at the ports] saw the sea, they shouted loudly and cried out, men and women, great and small, in their prayers demanding mercy of God.[44]

Most of these exiles encountered dreadful misfortune. Some drowned when their overcrowded ships sank; others turned back and were forcibly converted; and still others reached the north African coast but were captured by Moors, robbed, and then either killed or sold into slavery. (More than a few Jews died when their captors sliced open their abdomens searching for gold coins some had swallowed for safekeeping.)

Isabella and Ferdinand receive the advice of Catholic Church leaders while overseeing the mass deportation of Spanish Jews.

41

The Inquisition next turned on Spanish Muslims. In January 1492 Isabella and Ferdinand, after several years of relentless attacks, had managed to gain control of the Moorish kingdom of Granada, giving them control of all of Spain except Navarre in the north. Although some Moors had left, many had reluctantly stayed, hoping the Spanish would treat them fairly. This hope was dashed when, beginning in 1499, Spanish churchmen and troops initiated a program of forced conversions. In an effort to eliminate the supposed source of the "heresy," namely Muslim teachings, Spanish monks and soldiers cruelly confiscated and burned all Arabic books, both religious and secular.

Isabella's Setting Sun

The year 1492 turned out to be a busy and momentous one for Isabella's new Spain. It marked not only the conquest of Granada and the Jewish expulsion edict but also the start of Columbus's first voyage to the New World. For five years prior, Columbus had tried repeatedly to convince the queen to back him in an attempt to reach India by sailing west and thereby to partake of the fabled riches of that distant land. She finally agreed after one of her advisers argued that such a voyage might end up spreading Christianity to Indian "infidels" and thereby glorifying God and the Catholic Church. Columbus never reached India, of course, since North America got in his way, and the church gained few new converts. But the financial gains that came from opening the New World to settlement and exploitation were enormous and made Spain one of Europe's (and indeed the world's) leading nations almost overnight.

But while the sun was rising on a new Spanish empire, it was setting on the monarch who had made that empire possible. Illness began to take a terrible toll on the royal family. First, in October 1497, Isabella's beloved son, Juan, died of a raging fever at age nineteen. The grief-stricken queen and her husband held out hope that the prince's widow, who was then pregnant, would bear them a grandson who might rule over a united Spain in Juan's stead. Unfortunately, the baby was stillborn. Isabella's own health then steadily deteriorated and she died (possibly of cancer, for her doctors described a large tumor) on November 26, 1504. Ferdinand expressed his deep sorrow in a letter penned that day to Castilian high officials:

> On this day, Our Lord has taken away Our Serene Highness Queen Isabella, my dear and beloved wife, and al-

42

Christopher Columbus, accompanied by a group of Native Americans, greets Queen Isabella after returning from his first voyage to the New World.

though her death is the greatest suffering that I could ever have in this life . . . seeing that she died as a saint and a Catholic as she had lived her life, I hope that our Lord has her in his glory and that for her it is a better and more eternal kingdom than the ones she has had on earth.[45]

Soon after Isabella's death, Ferdinand became regent in Castile. In 1512 he invaded and annexed Navarre, completing the Spanish unification he and his wife had begun with their marriage years before. Thereafter, a true sense of national identity steadily took hold in Spain. In the fullness of time, as happens to all empires, the vast Spain of the great age of exploration eventually shrank and disintegrated. But the Spanish homeland remains united to this day, a nation proud of its heritage, including its birth long ago in the romantic vision of an obstinate teenage girl.

CHAPTER 4

Elizabeth I:
England's Loving Mother

Elizabeth, whom many of her subjects affectionately called "Bess," was one of the most charismatic and influential rulers ever to lead a nation. Her long reign (1558–1603) became known as the Elizabethan Age in her honor. It was a highly restless and spectacularly fruitful period for England and for much of the rest of Europe. In many crucial areas, especially religion, philosophy, politics, science, and literature, new ideas came into conflict with those of the older established order, the last vestiges of medieval society. Not long before Elizabeth ascended the English throne, Europe had witnessed the breakup of feudalism; the invention of gunpowder, the mariner's compass (making it possible to navigate the open seas), and printing; and the advent of the Copernican system of astronomy (showing that the sun, not the earth, lay at the center of the known universe). These and other new conceptions profoundly affected human thought and initiated widespread intellectual, social, and economic upheavals and transformations.

Partly because of these changes, and partly because of Elizabeth's forceful and largely constructive policies, England rose to greatness during her reign. It had long been a small kingdom on Europe's periphery, with minimal influence beyond its immediate neighbor, France. But under Elizabeth, England rapidly began building a global maritime empire, as Sir Francis Drake, Sir John Hawkins, and other adventurous English captains helped to turn the sea lanes into great highways for England's growing naval power. England's command of the waves brought it commercial success and its ports and cities became bustling centers of high finance, social life, and the arts. This highly fertile creative atmosphere stimulated a remarkable generation of writers and playwrights, including immortals like William Shakespeare, Ben Jonson, and Christopher Marlowe. In another immortal highlight of the age, Elizabeth's forces defeated those of Catholic Spain, ensuring that England would thereafter remain a Protestant nation. Near the end of her reign, the speaker of Parliament's House of Commons spoke sincerely on behalf of a grateful nation when he publicly told her:

> It is a wonder to other countries, amid the tempestuous storms they be tossed with, to behold the calm and halcyon [peaceful and happy] days of England, that possess a princess in whom dwells such undaunted courage without all dismay of any womanish fear, such singular wisdom . . . and such sincere justice. . . . I do wonderfully fear [that] it will hereafter be said of you, "The honor and happiness of peace among us of England, after so many and so great interruptions of it, began and ended in Your Majesty." [46]

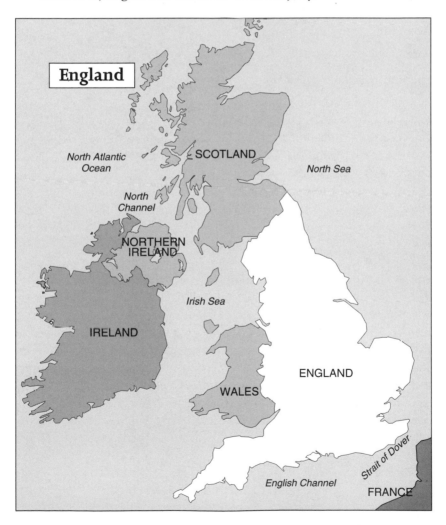

England

North Atlantic
Ocean

SCOTLAND

North Sea

North
Channel

NORTHERN
IRELAND

Irish Sea

IRELAND

ENGLAND

WALES

Strait of Dover

English Channel

FRANCE

Young Elizabeth and Her Siblings

Elizabeth came into the world on September 7, 1533. The only child of the union between England's King Henry VIII (reigned 1509–1547), head of the noble House of Tudor, and his second wife, Anne Boleyn, Elizabeth was in a sense a product of the religious turmoil that would later help define her reign. In order to divorce his first wife, Catherine of Aragon, who had failed to bear him a son, Henry had broken with the papacy, thereby separating the Church of England from the Catholic Church. The king was disappointed again when his second marriage brought forth a daughter instead of a male heir. When Elizabeth was only three, he charged her mother with adultery, had her beheaded, and declared that their marriage had been invalid. Thus, the child who would grow up to be viewed by millions as England's loving mother, herself grew up without her mother and was, technically speaking, illegitimate.[47]

Queen Elizabeth I as a young woman. An avid and quick learner, she became fluent in several languages and developed a love for reading.

Elizabeth's childhood was not an unhappy one, however. Henry's last wife, Catherine Parr, became almost like a mother to her; and the young girl held much affection for her half brother, Edward Tudor, Henry's only son (by his third wife, Jane Seymour). Elizabeth received an excellent education and learned to read Latin and Greek with facility, as well as speak fluent French, Italian, and Spanish. Eventually she acquired the habit of reading history books for several hours almost every day. Her tutor, Roger Ascham, claimed he had never before encountered a pupil who could so quickly comprehend and remember so much information.

When Henry died in 1547, Edward, then age ten, ascended the throne as Edward VI. Under his regents, Edward Seymour and John Dudley, young Edward maintained the Church of England's Protestant status, and the *Book of Common Prayer,* an English translation of important church rituals, was published during his reign. In 1552, however, Edward fell ill and in the following year he died. His half sister, the short-sighted and narrow-minded Mary Tudor, inherited the throne and tried to bring Catholicism back to the country. Her short reign was noteworthy for her condemnation of some three hundred Protestants to death by burning. In 1558 she died of ovarian cancer, miserable and having taken to wearing armor out of fear of assassination.

Elizabeth's Magic Veil

When Elizabeth Tudor succeeded her half sister as Elizabeth I on November 17, 1558, the outlook for her reign and for England's future in general seemed bleak. Hatred between Catholics and Protestants was rampant, prices were high, wages were low, and unemployment was on the increase. Pessimism was widespread because few of the kingdom's inhabitants realized at the time how formidable and talented a personality had taken control of the nation.

Elizabeth (pictured) inherited the throne from her sister, Mary Tudor, who had tried but failed to reinstate Catholicism.

At the age of twenty-five, Elizabeth was physically impressive—tall, with reddish gold hair and a confident, regal bearing. But could she govern boldly and effectively?

The answer came in short order. After becoming queen, Elizabeth immediately named the capable Sir William Cecil as her chief minister and together they hammered out a plan they hoped would settle the country's religious question. At their lead, Parliament quickly, if somewhat reluctantly, passed a series of bills early in 1559, collectively referred to as the Elizabethan Settlement.[48] One bill established Elizabeth as "Supreme Governor" of the realm's spiritual matters; another restored the *Book of Common Prayer*, which Mary had suppressed; and others officially declared the Church of England a Protestant entity.

The management style Elizabeth displayed in these opening months of her reign became one of her hallmarks. She showed an innate ability to choose as her advisers and ministers men of exceptional talent and ability, so much so that she rarely found it necessary to dismiss them. Besides the masterful statesman Cecil, these included, among many others, Sir Christopher Hatton, lord chancellor of the realm, who often skillfully bent Parliament to Elizabeth's will; and Sir Walter Raleigh, the gifted soldier, historian, and navigator. Elizabeth also understood how to manipulate powerful people and institutions and public opinion in general without sacrificing her popularity. As Elizabethan scholar Lacey B. Smith observes:

> The greatness of Elizabeth's accomplishment lay in the sixth sense that led her to demand of her subjects only what they wished to give, in the talent of bestowing upon the socially prominent elements of society the fruits of office while depriving them of the power of government, and in the artistry by which she enveloped functions of state in a magic veil of pomp and circumstance.[49]

Though generally popular as a ruler, Elizabeth was frequently difficult to get along with on a personal level, and more than one observer remarked how her closest associates "feared" her temper. When stressed or annoyed, she could be selfish and ungrateful. And she was known at times to slap both ladies-in-waiting and ministers across the face when they raised her ire. What is more, she was notoriously vain. As Lacey says:

> She thrived on—and demanded—constant compliments . . . and gifts from those around her . . . accepting the grossest and most obvious flattery with relish, and took it amiss when her ladies in waiting seemed more interested in an attractive courtier than in herself. . . . Even when her beauty had gone and her hair had faded, her passion for sumptuous clothes and costly jewelry to "set off" her figure and face did not abate.[50]

Elizabeth possessed qualities that magnetically drew men to her; thus, she had many suitors (although she never married). One of her major modern biographers, Elizabeth Jenkins, points out that, to handsome and accomplished men, the queen was often

> brilliantly responsive; she met with comprehension and sympathy a wide range of [their] interests; anything, indeed, that interested the men around her, interested her. . . . She rode so fast that it alarmed the Master of the

Horse responsible for her safety, and danced and walked as if she could never get enough of rapid motion. But, active . . . though she was, one of her strongest claims on men was her dependence on them. She excited those whose ambitions and hopes were the same as her own, and she made them understand that she could not do without them.[51]

Dealing with Threats to Her Throne

Among the many talented, adventurous, and creative men whom Elizabeth inspired and encouraged were navigators, explorers, writers, playwrights, composers, and educators. In 1581 navigator Francis Drake returned to England after successfully sailing around the world, challenging Spanish and Portuguese domination of the oceans. To show her appreciation, the queen knighted Drake. Following his lead, other English ship captains boldly took to the seas, initiating an age of foreign settlement and economic expansion for the kingdom. At the same time, Elizabeth often paid playwrights to stage productions of their works both at court and at universities such as those at Oxford and Cambridge. A staunch patron of education as well as the arts, she provided generous financial support for the universities themselves and for all manner of scholarly endeavor.

This golden age for adventurers and creators constituted one of the most important legacies of Elizabeth's reign. Of even greater impact, both in her own time and for later generations, was her ultimate solution of the religious-political question she had first addressed in the 1559 Elizabethan Settlement. Although this legislation had officially endorsed Protestantism over Catholicism in England, it had not eliminated religious hatred and rivalry. Much of Europe was still Catholic. And for a long time Elizabeth worried that the Catholic powers, led by perhaps the most fanatic of their number, Spain, might unite to force her from her throne. Catholicism also threatened Elizabeth's throne in another guise— that of her distant relative, Mary Stuart, also known as Mary, queen of Scots. The granddaughter of Henry VIII's sister, Margaret Tudor, and James IV of Scotland, Mary fled for sanctuary to England in 1568 when her Scottish subjects rebelled against her. A staunch Catholic, Mary became the focus of several anti-Protestant conspiracies against Elizabeth.

The Catholic issue came to a dramatic climax beginning in 1586. In that year Mary was found guilty of treason and sentenced to death; five months later, on February 1, 1587, Elizabeth signed the execution order (Mary was beheaded on February 8). Partly in response to Mary's demise and also because Elizabeth had recently sent aid to Dutch rebels attempting to break free of Spanish influence, King Philip II of Spain decided to depose Elizabeth by force and restore Catholicism to England. In July 1588 the seemingly invincible Spanish Armada, consisting of some 130 warships and troop transports, appeared in the English Channel. Through a combination of Spanish disorganization, an intrepid English fleet, and unexpected storms, the mighty invasion force met with disaster. "The Spanish Armada has had a terrible time of it," wrote a contemporary observer. "It is [now, after dreadful losses,] barely over 80 vessels strong and the English are after it with 250 [warships] and firing heavily with a favorable wind. The Spaniards have had no rest day or night for sixteen to eighteen days." [52] European heads of state were thoroughly stunned by the English victory and impressed by Elizabeth's resoluteness and

A grim Elizabeth agrees to sign the death warrant for her distant relative, Mary, queen of Scots.

courage in overcoming such tremendous odds. Even the pope, Sixtus V, who had opposed Elizabeth and helped to finance the Armada, could not restrain his admiration. "What a valiant woman," he remarked. "It is a pity that Elizabeth and I cannot marry; our children would have ruled the whole world." [53]

England Orphaned

The Armada's defeat and Elizabeth's continued opposition to Spain did not eliminate the Spanish as competitors for control of the seas. But her tough stance in wartime, along with her promotion of overseas exploration, helped to establish England as a world power. These and other accomplishments won her the gratitude and love of most of her subjects; and evidence suggests that the feeling was mutual. Although politically motivated, for instance, her famous "golden speech," delivered to Parliament in 1601, shortly before her death, contained touches of heartfelt sincerity. "My heart was never set on worldly goods," she stated,

> but only for my subjects' good. . . . There will never be a queen [who will] sit in my seat with more zeal to my country, care for my subjects,

Elizabeth's greatest and most lasting contribution to England was to establish it as a world power.

> and that will sooner with willingness venture her life for your good and safety, than myself. . . . And though you have had and may have many princes more mighty and wise sitting in this seat, yet you never had nor shall have any that will be more careful and loving. [54]

A majority of Elizabeth's subjects, rich and poor, remembered these words fondly on the day of her passing, March 24, 1603. [55] As one of her modern biographers, the late Katherine Anthony, memorably remarked, "The country mourned her like an orphan," for in a very real sense, "her reign was a marriage, and the nation was her child." [56]

CHAPTER 5

Catherine the Great: An Iron Will and a Restless Heart

"Nature seemed to have formed the Princess for the highest state of human elevation,"[57] wrote a member of France's embassy to Russia in 1762. The "Princess" to whom the Frenchman referred was Catherine II, who had that year become empress of the vast and then still technologically and culturally backward nation of Russia. By the end of her reign in 1796, Russia had undergone a major transformation, putting it on a par with other developed European nations of the day. Russian society (at least its well-to-do elements) had become far more literate and cultured, agriculture and industry had been significantly modernized, and the country's military and political power had increased enormously. These achievements earned Catherine the nickname of "the Great" both in her own and later times.

That Catherine was able to accomplish so much is a testament to her intelligence, energy, and diligence, all of which she possessed in abundance. One of Russia's foremost modern historians, Nicholas Riasanovsky, sums up her qualities:

> A woman quite out of the ordinary, the empress possessed . . . a natural ability to administer and govern, a remarkable practical sense . . . and an iron will. Along with her determination went courage and optimism: Catherine believed that she could prevail over all obstacles, and more often than not events proved her right. Self-control, skill in discussion and propaganda, and a clever handling of men and circumstances to serve her ends were additional assets . . . [along with] a constant, urgent drive to excel in everything and bring everything under one's control. . . . Russia had acquired a sovereign who worked day and night, paying personal attention to all kinds of matters, great and small.[58]

Yet if her qualities can be called great, so can her faults. Catherine's ambition, determination, and need to transform and control sometimes bordered on obsession and ruthlessness. Some (although certainly not all) of her contemporaries felt that she lacked charity and human sympathy. And she was very vain and self-centered. Moreover, she was unable to find permanent happiness in her private life. She was notorious for having numerous lovers over the course of her long reign (twenty-one are documented, but there were probably more); and this succession of mostly failed relationships reveals the layers of insecurity and sadness beneath her grand, colorful, and seemingly confident exterior.

The Route to the Throne

Catherine did not inherit the Russian throne directly, mainly because she was not Russian in the first place. She was born Sophie Friederike Auguste von Anhalt-Zerbst, the daughter of a prominent local nobleman in Stettin, a town in the German principality of Anhalt-Zerbst, on May 2, 1729. (She received her more familiar Russian name of Yekaterina Alekseyevna when she was accepted into the Russian Orthodox Church in 1744.) During her childhood her parents showed her little attention or affection. However, she was fortunate to have had a governess, a well-educated Frenchwoman named Babbete Cardel, who was patient and kind and introduced her to the works of important poets and playwrights. Thanks largely to this training, as Catherine matured, she became an eager devotee and patroness of writing and other arts.

Born in Germany, raised by a French governess, and later accepted into the Russian Orthodox Church, Catherine II had a uniquely international background.

Catherine's arduous route to the Russian throne began in 1739, when she was ten. The occasion was a casual meeting with her eleven-year-old second cousin, Peter Ulrich, a grandson of the great Russian czar Peter I ("the Great"), who had died in 1725. She was singularly unimpressed with the boy, whom she saw as dim-witted and boring. But in the next few years she increasingly saw that a relationship with him could be her ticket to potential wealth and power in the Russian court.

Since the days of the forceful and capable Peter I, that court had degenerated into a hotbed of petty jealousies and intrigues. In their own self-interests, the army and aristocracy repeatedly determined the royal succession, ensuring the rule of one unremarkable and untalented royal relative after another. These included Peter's wife, Catherine I (reigned 1725–1727); his grandson, Peter II (1727–1730); his niece, Anna (1730–1741); and his daughter, Elizabeth (1741–1762).

When Elizabeth died in 1762, Peter Ulrich and Catherine entered this succession. Peter and Catherine had married in 1745, when she was fifteen. By that time it was clear to all that he was mentally unbalanced and she lived a miserable existence with him for almost two decades until he succeeded Elizabeth as Czar Peter III. After only a few months on the throne, however, he was deposed when some nobles and the powerful royal guards staged a coup and hailed Catherine empress in his stead. She entered the capital, St. Petersburg, in triumph on June 30, 1762 (the formal coronation took place on September 22), and a few days later Peter died under somewhat mysterious circumstances.[59]

A Backward and Uncultured Country

It was not long before foreign ambassadors and other dignitaries, as well as Russians of all walks of life, realized that the new ruler was not made in the same mediocre mold as her several immediate predecessors. In the first place, she had a striking appearance, as remembered by a contemporary French diplomat, Claude de Rulhiere:

> Her figure is noble . . . her gait majestic; her person and deportment graceful in the highest degree. Her air is that of a sovereign. Every feature proclaims a superior character. . . . Her forehead is large and open. . . . Her mouth is sweetly fresh, and embellished by a singularly regular and beautiful set of teeth. . . . Her hair is chestnut-colored, and uncommonly fine; the eyebrows are dark brown; the eyes hazel, and extremely fascinating. . . . Loftiness is the true character of her physiognomy [physical appearance].[60]

In the years that followed, Catherine proved that she had the strong character and genuine talent to match her majestic bearing, as she gradually but steadily reformed Russian society, laws, and institutions. To appreciate the extent and importance of these reforms, one must consider how backward and uncultured (by prevailing European standards) the country was when she became its leader. The following revealing vignettes are from an eyewitness account by John Perry, an English engineer who paid an extended visit to Russia in the early 1700s:

> It was a very rare thing . . . to have found any man, even among the highest and most learned of the clergy, to have understood any language but their own; and as they were themselves void of learning, so they were wary and cautious to keep out all means that might bring it in [particularly books], lest their ignorance should be discovered. . . . There is nothing more common than to have both the people and the priest, too, go to church on a holiday in the morning and get drunk in the afternoon . . . and so far from being accounted a scandal to be drunk [in public], that . . . even women of distinction and fashion will [admit] that they have been very drunk. . . . It is a thing common in Russia [for husbands] to beat wives in a most barbarous manner, very often so unhumanly that they die . . . [and some of these] wives murder their husbands in revenge . . . on which occasion there is a law made, that when they murder their husbands, they are set alive in the ground, standing upright, with the earth filled about them . . . till they are starved to death; which is a common sight in that country.[61]

Catherine addressed such public drunkenness, excessive cruelty, and murder, along with many other social problems, in laws and decrees issued throughout her reign. She began by setting up the Legislative Commission, made up of over five hundred delegates from all walks of life, between 1766 and 1767. The Commission's goal was to identify the problems and draw up legal reforms. As an initial guideline, Catherine gave the delegates the *Instructions*, much of which she had written herself—a set of ideas inspired by France's Charles de Montesquieu and other liberal philosophers of the European intellectual movement that became known as the Enlightenment. Although the Commission itself did not produce a comprehensive law code, Catherine later drew on its findings in enacting individual statutes and other reforms on a periodic basis.

Compromise and Reform

The Enlightenment, which was characterized by its appeal to human reason, religious toleration, newly discovered scientific

Catherine greets visiting French philosopher Denis Diderot (1713–1784), editor of the renowned Encyclopedia, *a compendium of general knowledge. She was long an enthusiastic supporter of scholars, educators, and thinkers.*

facts, and basic human rights, remained a major force shaping Catherine's thinking. The key to understanding her character is knowing that she fancied herself as highly enlightened, both as a person and a ruler. This is clearly revealed in her credo, a written tract expressing her moral ideals (which she wrote to herself and never published). "Study mankind," she began,

> Search for true merit, be it at the other end of the world, for usually it is modest and retiring. . . . Have confidence

in those who have the courage to contradict you if necessary and who place more value on your reputation than on your favor. Be gentle, humane, accessible, compassionate and liberal-minded: do not let your grandeur prevent you from condescending with kindness toward the small and putting yourself in their place. . . . Behave so that the kind love you, the evil fear you, and all respect you. Preserve in yourself those qualities of spirit which form the character of the honest man, the great man and the hero. . . . I swear by Providence to stamp these words in my heart and in the hearts of those who will read them after me.[62]

Catherine believed in these ideals throughout her reign. Unfortunately, she often found that acting on them was not as easy as she had envisioned. She faced the daunting task of fairly and effectively ruling a vast, backward country riddled with severe social and economic problems and in large degree controlled by powerful and entrenched special-interest groups, most notably the aristocracy and the army. Thus, she had to learn to compromise. In 1785, for instance, she issued the Charter of the Nobility, which guaranteed the aristocrats numerous rights and privileges. Here, she bowed to the reality that in Russia the nobles had more influence and control over the army than the monarch; and without the loyalty of the army, she could not govern the nation and attempt to institute needed reforms.

A Book-Friendly Ruler

Most of these reforms were, if not sweeping, certainly significant and helped propel Russia into Europe's social, economic, and cultural mainstream. Catherine reorganized local government, allowing educated property owners to run towns. And she established the Free Economic Society (1765), which encouraged modernization of agriculture and industry and promoted trade, land use, and expansion of the small Russian middle class. She also commissioned many new and stately buildings, including a palace, a theater, the Academy of Sciences, and the State Bank. These and others replaced the mostly primitive structures of old Russia and stimulated a golden age of architecture and construction.

Of special and long-lasting significance, Catherine made books, once scarce in Russia, much more readily available, thereby greatly stimulating education and scholarship. In 1768 she set up the Translators' Commission, which itself published 154 books in its first twelve years. She also authorized the installation of several new government-owned printing presses; and in 1783 she granted private persons the right to set up their own presses. In conjunction with these efforts, the enlightened empress encouraged poets and playwrights (as well as actors, musicians, and other artists), launched a new literary magazine (titled *All Sorts,* which she edited herself), and even wrote plays of her own.[63]

Catherine's foreign policy was in many ways as vigorous as her domestic programs. She continued and completed the drive, begun by previous Russian leaders, to achieve warm-water ports (the nation had cold-water ports on the Baltic Sea but none along the Black Sea in the south). In two wars fought against Turkey (1768–1774 and 1787–1792), Russia secured the Crimea, the large peninsula that projects into the northern Black Sea. Catherine also won free access to the Bosporus Strait (on the sea's southern flank), opening up new trade routes for her nation. In addition, she took part, along with other European rulers, in the partition (division) of Poland, which brought much new territory under Russian control.

Catherine's sympathy and generosity toward the public earned her the nickname "Little Mother."

"She Took Pleasure in Her Work"

It is ironic that, outside of Russia, Catherine is perhaps best remembered not for these impressive domestic and foreign achievements, but for her personal affairs. This is unfortunate because most of the stories in this vein, many of them initiated by her enemies or gossipmongers, are exaggerated or untrue. She did in fact have many lovers; however, she was not a sexual seductress, as often depicted, but essentially a sad and lonely woman searching for a perfect love that always eluded her. "If as a young woman," she wrote, "I had got a husband whom I could have loved, I would have remained forever faithful to him. My trouble is that my heart cannot rest content even for one hour without love."[64] This remark was contained in a note written to the Russian soldier and statesman Grigory Potemkin (1739–1791), her favorite companion; some historians believe they may have been secretly married, but supporting evidence is scarce.

An aging Catherine poses with a book to symbolize the importance of and her love for learning.

Catherine died as a result of a massive stroke. On November 14, 1796, per her usual custom, she rose at 6:00 A.M., had several cups of strong coffee, and began to work on a stack of royal correspondence. Later in the morning her valet found her lying unconscious in her private chamber. She died two days later. A few years before, after the death of her beloved friend Potemkin had forced her to face her own mortality, she had written her own epitaph. Surprisingly modest for so majestic a ruler, it remains a testament to her many good intentions, even if she was never able to fulfill them all. It concludes with the following description:

> On the throne of Russia she wanted to do what was good for her country and tried to bring happiness, liberty, and prosperity to her subjects. . . . She had a republican spirit and a kind heart. She was sociable by nature. She made many friends. She took pleasure in her work. She loved the arts.[65]

CHAPTER 6

Victoria: "The Grandmother of Europe"

⌐20 June 1837. I was awoke at 6 o'clock by Mamma, who told me that the Archbishop of Canterbury and Lord Conyngham [a high government official] were here, and wished to see me. I got out of bed and went into my sitting-room (only in my dressing gown), and *alone,* and saw them. . . . [They told] me that my poor Uncle, the King, was no more, and had expired at 12 minutes past 2 this morning, and consequently that I am *Queen.*[66]

This was how the eighteen-year-old British princess named Victoria described the death of her uncle, King William IV, and her accession as queen. She could not have known at the time that that day marked the beginning of a sixty-three-year reign, the longest in British history.⌐

Nor could the then nervous young woman have guessed that her years as queen would become known as the Victorian Age. One of Britain's most famous eras, it has come to be associated with traditional values such as hard work, thrift, strict morality, and veneration of family and homeland. Victoria conducted herself always as a model for these virtues, even if the age itself did not always conform to them. The first few decades of her reign witnessed the rapid growth of industry, huge increases in population, the rise to prominence of the British middle class, and much material prosperity. Proud of their past and optimistic about their future, the British, somewhat naively and arrogantly, came to see their conservative customs and values as "right" and "superior."

In the last few decades of Victoria's reign, by contrast, as new inventions and technology multiplied and spread, the pace of change and of daily life became much more rapid, *too* rapid for many people. The nation began to suffer widespread unemployment and other economic problems, and new scientific discoveries (including Charles Darwin's theory of evolution) began to undermine long-held religious teachings. As a result, many people became disillusioned with society's traditional values and institutions.

Victoria's greatest achievement was to make the monarchy a kind of refuge for and preserver of these traditional, conservative British views and values. The times when the king or queen actually governed the country were long past. The nation's supreme legislature, Parliament, held the actual reigns of state and under royal rulers of lesser stature the monarchy might have fallen into disrepute and withered away. The stubborn and hardworking Victoria, however, transformed the monarchy into a dignified and popular institution, a proud symbol of Britain's imperial past. "In a rapidly-changing society," comments historian H. C. G. Matthew, the Victorian monarchy

When she sat for this early portrait, Victoria did not foresee that she would become queen, let alone enjoy a long reign.

seemed something of a fixed point, with its emphasis on family, continuity, and religion. . . . The obvious ordinariness of Victoria herself, her well-publicized sufferings . . . and the fact that she was a woman, old and often ill, pointed up the contrast between human frailty and the majesty of institutions, much increasing respect for the latter. The monarchy represented the timeless quality of [the] pre-industrial order. In an increasingly urbanized society, it balanced the Industrial Revolution: the more urban Britain became, the more stylized, ritualized, and popular became its monarchy.[67]

As Stubborn as She Was Poised

The tiny (only five-foot-tall) but forceful woman who in a sense created Britain's modern ceremonial monarchy was born on May 24, 1819, at Kensington Palace in London. She was the only child of Edward, duke of Kent, a son of King George III (reigned 1760–1820), and Mary Louisa Victoria, daughter of a duke of the German principality of Saxe-Coburg. At birth Victoria was rated only fifth in line to succeed the still living George III, her grandfather. Three of her uncles and her own father stood before her in the succession, so everyone looked on her chances at becoming queen as extremely remote. This situation changed markedly over the course of her childhood, however. Her father died in 1820 (less than a year after she was born); six days later George III died and one uncle succeeded him as George IV; in 1827 another uncle died; in 1830 George IV died, and her last remaining uncle succeeded him as William IV.

Thus, when William IV died on June 30, 1837, Victoria, having defied the odds of fate and chance, became queen of Great Britain and Ireland. Later that day, the eighteen-year-old made a very positive first impression on the chief ministers of state when she met with them in her first public appearance. One of them later recalled:

> Never was anything like the first impression she produced, or the chorus of praise and admiration which is raised about her manner and behavior, and certainly not without justice. . . . After she had read her speech, and taken and signed the oath of the security of the Church . . . I saw her blush up to the eyes . . . and this was the only sign of emotion which she evinced. . . . She went through the whole ceremony . . . with perfect calmness and self-possession, but at the same time with a graceful modesty and propriety particularly interesting and ingratiating.[68]

As a young queen, Victoria was restrained and proper but also stubborn, as shown by her unyielding stance during the "Bedchamber Crisis."

It soon became clear, and perhaps a bit vexing to these statesmen, that the new monarch was as forceful and stubborn as she was graceful and poised. By the time she became queen, the monarchy had already evolved into a mostly ceremonial yet still quite influential entity. The elected members of Parliament, led by the prime minister, ran the country and empire; however, the crown, still a potent symbol of power and majesty, could exert moderate influence on governmental affairs by lending public support to one political party or administration.

Victoria's use of this sort of partisan support became a heated issue less than two years after her accession. The prime minister, Lord Melbourne, a charming and worldly elderly gentleman, had taken her under his wing and become a kind of personal adviser and political tutor. In long sessions in palace drawing rooms, he broadened her rather limited knowledge of the world, instilled in her a great deal of confidence, and the two became close friends.

What led to trouble was that Melbourne, like Victoria's father, belonged to the popular Whig party. He surrounded the queen with ladies-in-waiting from Whig families, ensuring that she would remain a Whig partisan. When he resigned for political reasons in May 1839, Sir Robert Peel, leader of the Conservative party, was expected to take power as prime minister. But he objected to the continued presence at court of Victoria's Whig ladies, the wives and daughters of his political opponents. She surprised many when she stubbornly refused to replace them, precipitating the so-called "bedchamber crisis." The upshot was that Peel refused to take office and the queen had to recall Melbourne, who presided over an unstable and unproductive political climate for two more years. Some sixty years later, having matured personally and having come to admire and respect Peel, she admitted, "I was very young then, and perhaps I should act differently if it was all to be done again."[69]

Albert, Her "Angel"

Indeed, in time Victoria came to adopt a policy of relative neutrality in political matters, which had the inevitable effect of further decreasing the monarchy's effective authority and making it more ceremonial than it already was. The person who influenced her more than anyone else in this and her other political attitudes was her husband, Albert. He was her first cousin and a prince of Saxe-Coburg. In October 1839, as part of a matchmaking scheme engineered by one of Victoria's relatives, Albert arrived at Windsor Castle for a visit and immediately charmed the young queen beyond her wildest expectations. "It was with some emotion," she later wrote, "that I beheld Albert—who is *beautiful* . . . so excessively handsome, such beautiful blue eyes, an exquisite nose . . . a beautiful figure, broad in the shoulders and a fine waist.[70] Five days later, she proposed to him (because of his lower rank, he could not speak first), and he accepted. Their wedding took place on February 10, 1840, and the next day she penned this note to a relative:

> I write to you from here [Windsor], the happiest, happiest Being that ever existed. Really, I do not think it *possible* for anyone in the world to be *happier,* or *as* happy as I am. He is an Angel, and his kindness and affection for me is really touching. To look in those dear eyes, and that dear sunny face, is enough to make me adore him. What I can do to make him happy will be my greatest delight.[71]

Prince Albert, a German noble and Victoria's first cousin, remained her husband, close friend, and confidant until his untimely death in 1861.

Victoria's love and admiration for Albert (and his for her) never dimmed in the roughly two decades they had together. He was her friend, confidant, and often performed the duties of a personal secretary. A very conservative and straitlaced individual, his prim and proper traits and opinions rubbed off on and remained with her always, in many ways helping to define the conservative image of the age. They had nine children together and many grandchildren. Because so many of their grandchildren ended up marrying foreign rulers and in a sense populating Europe's royal families, posterity has accorded Victoria the affectionate nickname of "the Grandmother of Europe."[72]

Albert was a major guiding force behind one of the greatest and most famous achievements of Victoria's reign—the 1851 Great Exhibition of the Works of Industry of All Nations. A kind of world's fair celebrating the fruits of the Industrial Revolution, the Great Exhibition displayed over one hundred thousand inventions and other objects in the Crystal Palace, a magnificent 1,848-foot-long glass structure erected in London's Hyde Park by the amateur architect Joseph Paxton. Victoria herself later described the opening day's festivities as the *greatest* day in our history, the *most beautiful* and *imposing* and *touching* spectacle ever seen, and the triumph of my beloved Albert. . . . Albert's dearest name is immortalized with this *great* conception. . . . The triumph is *immense*, for up to the *last hour*, the difficulties . . . were immense; but Albert's . . . patience, firmness, and energy surmounted all.[73]

The Great Exhibition, which loudly proclaimed Britain's status as a world economic power, was a resounding success, drawing some 6 million visitors and turning a handsome profit.

Her Majesty, Mrs. Brown

Albert's presence and influence, of which the Great Exhibition was in a sense a public commemoration, marked the zenith of Victoria's life and reign. She was, understandably, emotionally devastated when Albert died unexpectedly of typhoid fever in 1861. "For me, all is over," she wrote a few months after her loss.

I lived only through him, the heavenly Angel. He was my whole being, my life, my soul, yes, even my conscience! . . . Disheartened, and without interest or pleasure, I try to continue my dark and gloomy life alone. . . . I try to comfort myself by knowing that he is always near me, although invisible, and that our future union will be even more perfect and eternal.[74]

Thereafter, the queen remained in what was essentially a state of mourning for the rest of her long life. For the most part, she withdrew from the world, made few public appearances, and spent most of her time in her houses on the Isle of Wight (off the southern coast, opposite the city of Portsmouth) and in the Scottish Highlands. Her popularity declined for some years, partly because the public liked its monarch to be more visible. But there was also the taint of scandal that derived from her controversial relationship with a Scottish highlander named John Brown from the late 1860s through the early 1880s. Hired as a servant, Brown became Victoria's close friend and confidant, much to the displeasure of most of her relatives and the delight of the gossip mill and press. One nobleman reported:

The Queen has taken a fancy to a certain Scotch servant, by name Brown: will have no one else to wait upon her, makes him drive her out alone in a pony carriage, walk with, rather than after her, gives orders through him . . .

allows him access to her such as no one else has [including her bedchamber], and in various ways distinguishes him beyond what is customary or fitting in that position. [The affair has] become a joke throughout Windsor, where H[er] M[ajesty] is talked of as "Mrs. Brown": and if it lasts the joke will grow into a scandal.[75]

No one knows just how intimate the queen's relationship with Brown became. In all likelihood it remained always platonic; nevertheless, it was apparently in most other ways nearly as close as the one she had enjoyed with her husband. When Brown died in

This famous photo shows Victoria with her personal attendant, John Brown. Their controversial private relationship became a favorite topic of gossip.

1883, she wrote to a grandson, "I have lost my *dearest best* friend whom no one in *this World* can *ever* replace. . . . My grief is unbounded, dreadful, & I know not how to bear it." [76]

Like Another World

Victoria continued to live mainly in seclusion after Brown's passing, but she still avidly kept up with the political scene, in which she thought the monarchy should always play some role. Though she attempted to be impartial, she still had her favorite politicians and ministers and did not attempt to hide it when she disliked someone. When the distinguished liberal prime minister William Gladstone died in 1898, for example, her first response was, "I never liked him. How can I say I'm sorry?" [77] Victoria was not only coldly blunt, says the popular biographer of English royalty Christopher Hibbert, but "difficult, demanding, and capricious" as well.

> Her intellect was limited, but she had an astonishingly good memory. She was hardworking, well-informed, and shrewd. Her judgements, however, were never tentative, never in doubt. Incapable of lying . . . she was also incapable of understanding that there were degrees of reprehensibility [badness]. [To her] a thing was right or it was wrong; a person was good or bad; and once her mind was made up, she had absolute confidence in her opinion. [78]

Victoria remained opinionated until her death on January 22, 1901, at the age of eighty-one. She had presided over Britain's rapid modernization and entry into the twentieth century. Indeed, as personified by the Great Exhibition, sweeping social and economic change was the underlying theme of the Victorian Age. A London merchant summed it up memorably in this diary entry made the day after Victoria's death:

> The streets were crowded as usual. But there seemed an unusual hush over the traffic and the people I passed looked at me as though I were in need of their sympathy, as though we have shared a loss in the family, as, I suppose, in a way we have. I fell to thinking . . . of all the changes I have seen. Not just in the way we live but in the way we think about things. . . . I wonder what our sons and grandsons will make of it all. It will be like reading about another world. [79]

CHAPTER 7

Golda Meir: The Woman Who Made Israel Possible

Golda Meir, known to millions of people around the world simply and often affectionately as "Golda," was one of the best-known and most influential women of the twentieth century. She served as Israel's foreign minister (1956–1966) and its first woman prime minister (1969–1974). Her most significant and lasting contribution, however, was the pivotal role she played in the long struggle of modern Jews to establish a national state in Palestine (the region lying along the eastern Mediterranean coast). Through her tireless fund-raising and speech-making efforts over the course of many years, she rallied a great deal of the financial and moral support that proved crucial to Israel's founding in 1948. In the years that followed, Golda continued to work tirelessly, focusing nearly all of her energies on strengthening and defending the new Jewish homeland. In time, most Israelis came to see her as a national treasure and called her Golda *shelanu,* "our Golda." A noted biographer writes, "This was a woman who lived in a state of emergency, paid her dues, earned her greatness. Out of her strength, she helped create a nation; out of her spirit, she helped mold a people. If Israel had a voice in the world, it was the voice of Golda." [80]

Seeking a Better Life

In reality, Golda had not just one voice, but many. Though Jewish by ethnicity and religion, she held many nationalities and spoke several languages during her long and productive life. That life began on May 3, 1898, in Kiev, on the Dnieper River in the Russian Ukraine. Her father, Moshe Yitzhak Mabovitch, was a Russian Jewish carpenter and cabinetmaker, and her mother, Bluma Naiditch, was the daughter of a tavern keeper. Of Moshe's and Bluma's nine children, all died of smallpox, typhoid fever, and other ailments except for Golda and two sisters— Sheyna and Tzipke.

St. Petersburg

Moscow

Vitebsk

RUSSIAN
EMPIRE

Baltic Sea

Berlin

GERMANY

Kiev

Poltava

UKRAINE

Krakow

Elizavetgrad

SWITZERLAND

Vienna

Budapest

Kishinev

Basel

AUSTRIA-HUNGARY

Odessa

ROMANIA

Black Sea

SERBIA

ITALY

Constantinople

The Jewish Pale of Settlement
in Russia, 1827–1917

OTTOMAN EMPIRE

SYRIA

When Golda was a child, anti-Semitism, or hatred of Jews, was rampant in most of Russia, as it was in many other parts of Europe. Most of Russia's 5 million Jews were forced to live in substandard conditions in ghettos in a special zone called the Pale of Settlement, north of the Black Sea. Kiev lay outside the Pale of Settlement, which meant that Jews needed a special permit to live there. Moshe had obtained a permit by making a finely crafted chess table, proving that he could be an asset to the community.

But Moshe's skills, honesty, and other qualities did not matter to most non-Jews. Jewish men, women, and children were routinely beaten, terrorized, and killed, a deplorable situation that finally convinced Golda's father that he must move his family to a safer land. In 1903 he sold his tools to raise the cash needed to buy a ticket to the United States. Bluma and the girls moved temporarily to Pinsk, a mostly Jewish town inside the Pale of Settlement, where they lived and worked in her father's tavern while waiting for Moshe to send for them. He was finally able to do so in 1906. At the age of eight Golda, along with her mother and sisters, traveled overland to Belgium and there boarded a ship bound for New York. "Going to America then was almost like going to the moon," Golda later recalled.

Perhaps if we had known that throughout Europe thousands of families like ours were on the move, headed toward what they, too, firmly believed would be, and was indeed, a better life in the New World, we would have been less frightened. But we knew nothing about the many women and children who were traveling then under similar conditions from countries like Ireland, Italy and Poland to join husbands and fathers in America, and we were very scared.[81]

On reaching New York, their journey was far from over. They then had to travel hundreds of miles westward to Milwaukee, Wisconsin, the prosperous American city where Moshe had settled. Golda was at first overwhelmed by how clean, modern, and friendly her new surroundings seemed compared to the unsafe squalor of the Pale of Settlement, but she adjusted quickly. She rapidly learned English and proved herself a good student at school.

"I Belonged in Palestine"

It was during these early years in the United States that Golda came to believe fervently that it was unfair for Jews to have to flee from one land to another in search of decent lives. For several decades various Jewish leaders and thinkers had advocated the establishment of a Jewish homeland in Palestine, the site of the ancient nation of Israel, land God had supposedly guaranteed the Jews.[82] Golda agreed about the need for a homeland, but she was motivated more by a sense of justice and need than by religious tradition. She later remembered:

> It was not a particularly religious household. My parents, of course, observed Jewish tradition. They kept a kosher kitchen and celebrated all the Jewish holidays and festivals. But religion as such—to the extent that it can be separated from tradition for Jews—played very little role in our lives. I can't remember as a child ever having thought very much about God or praying to a personal deity, although when I was older . . . I sometimes argued with my mother about religion. . . . As for the Jews being a chosen people, I never quite accepted that. It seemed, and it still seems to me, more reasonable to believe, not that God chose the Jews, but that the Jews were the first people that chose God, the first people in history to have done something truly revolutionary, and it was this choice that made them unique.[83]

Because of her commitment to helping Jews achieve a new Israel, as a young woman Golda took every opportunity to promote the idea. During World War I, when Jews in many parts of Europe were forced from their homes by various armies on the move, she stood on street corners and gave speeches condemning the violence and calling for a Jewish homeland.

During these war years, an event occurred that proved an important initial step in the realization of Golda's and other Jews' dreams of a new Israel. On November 2, 1917, Britain's foreign secretary, Arthur Balfour, briefly spelled out his nation's position concerning the future of Palestine, most of which the British had recently taken control. His statement, which became known as the Balfour Declaration, said in part, "His majesty's Government view with favor the establishment in Palestine of a national home for the Jewish people, and will use their best endeavors to facilitate the achievement of this object."[84] This policy was motivated more by self-interest than by sympathy and good fellowship. The British hoped that advocating a Jewish homeland would rally the support of wealthy American Jews to the Allied war cause; and that a pro-British Jewish state in Palestine would help guard the Suez Canal, which was vital to Britain's overseas empire.

Young Golda Meir, then Golda Mabovitch (back row, second from left), worked as a schoolteacher in Milwaukee during World War I.

Selfish or not, the British had opened a door on a new era for Jews everywhere. Various Jewish organizations began lobbying in earnest for the creation of a new homeland and one of these, Poalei Zion (or Labor Zionist Party), sent Golda on speech-making tours of the United States and Canada. It was in this same period (December 1917) that she met and married a sign painter named Morris Meyerson. In 1921 the young couple traveled to Palestine and settled in the town of Tel Aviv, which would in time become one of modern Israel's largest cities. "I believed absolutely that as a Jew I belonged in Palestine," [85] Golda later wrote.

Making Israel a Reality

At first Golda and Morris lived on a kibbutz, a small community in which the members share their belongings and earnings, where they planted trees, picked almonds, paved roads, and built houses. Three years later they moved to Jerusalem, the largest town in Palestine, where they had two children, Menachem and Sarah. Meanwhile, Golda became increasingly active in political activities. Working for the Histadrut, or Labor Federation, the central organization of Jewish Palestinian laborers, she gave speeches in the United States and other countries, describing and promoting the growing population of Jewish settlers in Palestine.

The issue of a Jewish homeland, long held on the back burner by the British and other nations, finally came to a head in the three years following World War II. That colossal conflict had witnessed the brutal extermination of millions of European Jews in Nazi death camps. To ensure their future survival, many Jews believed they had to have their own state and thousands of Jews began converging on Palestine. Various Arab countries and groups in the area objected and local fighting and bloodshed, which had existed on a small scale for decades, greatly intensified.

Golda knew that it would be impossible for the Jews to win this conflict and establish their own state without large quantities of arms and supplies, which were very expensive. Early in 1948 she traveled to the United States in a determined attempt to get the needed money. "The Jewish community in Palestine is going to fight to the very end," she declared in one of her speeches.

> If we have arms to fight with, we will fight with them. If not, we will fight with stones in our hands. . . . There is no Jew in Palestine who does not believe that finally we will be victorious. . . . Our problem is time. . . . The question

is what can we get immediately. And, when I say immediately, I do not mean next month. I do not mean two months from now. I mean now.[86]

At the end of her whirlwind two-month fund-raising tour, Golda returned to Palestine with the incredible sum of $50 million. The prominent Jewish leader David Ben-Gurion exclaimed, "Someday when history will be written, it will be said that there was a Jewish woman who got the money which made the state [of Israel] possible."[87]

Indeed, thanks in large part to Golda's efforts, the modern state of Israel came into being on May 14, 1948. On that day, in a speech heard around the globe, Ben-Gurion, who would become the new nation's first prime minister, asserted: "By virtue of our national and historic right and of the resolution of the General Assembly of the United Nations, [we] do hereby proclaim the establishment of a Jewish state in the Land of Israel—the State of Israel."[88] At that moment, "My eyes filled with tears, and my hands shook," Golda later recalled. "We had done it. We had brought the Jewish state into existence—and I, Golda Mabovitch Meyerson, had

Golda Meir as Israel's prime minister. In the late 1940s, she raised most of the money needed to back Israel's fight for statehood.

lived to see the day. Whatever happened now, whatever price any of us would have to pay for it, we had recreated the Jewish national home. The long exile was over."[89]

A Relentlessly Active Public Life

Golda had been right about the Israelis having to pay a price for their new homeland. Their Arab neighbors were determined to crush the Jewish state before it had a chance to firmly implant itself and almost immediately Israel found itself under attack. Many people around the world held out little hope for Ben-Gurion, Golda, and their people. U.S. secretary of defense James Forrestal

Israeli field guns blast away at Syrian forces during one of Israel's numerous fights with its Arab neighbors.

is said to have remarked, "It's a question of arithmetic. There are 45 million Arabs and 350,000 Jews, and the 45 million Arabs are going to push the 350,000 Jews right into the ocean. That's all there is to it." [90] The *New York Post* summed up the situation this way:

> Imagine an area of 8,000 square miles in all. Make it 270 miles long and seventy miles wide at its widest; border it on three sides with enemy nations, their armies totaling between 70,000 and 80,000 troops; place within it . . . people from more than fifty nations, whose last experience with self-rule dates back 1,887 years; sever its sea and air communications . . . give it a name, declare it independent—and you have the state of Israel, one minute past midnight, May 15, 1948.[91]

Despite the formidable odds against it, Israel survived this and several other conflicts with its neighbors in the years that followed. During these formative years for the new country, Golda continued to play a leading role. She served first as Israel's ambassador to Russia, her native land. Then, in 1949, Ben-Gurion asked her to become minister of labor. In that capacity she helped set up schools to teach new citizens trades, created jobs, and built roads and housing. By 1953 her office had produced fifty-two thousand temporary housing units, eighty-two thousand small apartments, and twelve hundred public buildings.

Astonishingly, these achievements marked only the beginning of Golda's official career. Golda became Israel's foreign minister in 1956. (At that time, Ben-Gurion asked her to take a Hebrew name, as many leading Jews had already done for symbolic and patriotic reasons. She chose Meir, meaning "to give light.") In 1965, now sixty-seven and weary from her relentlessly active public life, Golda retired (although she retained her seat in the Knesset, Israel's national legislature). However, when Prime Minister Levi Eshkol died in office in 1969, her compatriots called on her to serve still again; and on March 7 of that year she became Israel's prime minister.

The highlight of Golda's tenure as her nation's leader was the 1973 Yom Kippur War, fought against Israel's longtime enemies, Syria and Egypt. When Arab troops began massing on Israeli borders, Golda worried that an attack might be imminent. But her military advisers insisted that the Arabs were not preparing to fight and persuaded her not to call up the nation's defense forces. This turned out to be bad advice. The Arabs did attack and although Israel pushed them back and eventually won the war, over twenty-five hundred Israelis were killed. Amid protests, mostly from the opposition party in the Knesset, that bad judgment had caused unnecessary casualties, Golda no longer felt confident about governing. She resigned as prime minister on April 10, 1974.

Golda's failing health was undoubtedly another reason behind her decision to leave politics. In 1963 she had been diagnosed with cancer of the lymphatic system. And in 1973, while serving as prime minister, she had begun receiving radiation treatments (in secret, so as not to alarm the public). In all, she courageously fought the disease for fifteen years before it finally took her life on December 8, 1978. She was eighty years old. In a real sense, the modern state of Israel was her monument, for without her courage and diligence, it might never have come into existence. Golda remained proud and determined to the end. The last words of her autobiography read:

> [I] am indebted for what has been given to me from the time that I first learned about [the movement for a Jewish homeland] in a small room in Czarist Russia, all the way through to my half century here, where I have seen my five grandchildren grow up as free Jews in a country that is their own. Let no one anywhere have any doubts about this: Our children and our children's children will never settle for anything less.[92]

CHAPTER 8

Margaret Thatcher: Great Britain's Iron Lady

When, on November 28, 1990, Margaret Thatcher resigned her office as Britain's prime minister, one of the most powerful political positions in the modern world, she left behind several "firsts" and shattered records. To begin with, she was the first woman to lead a major political party (the Conservatives, or Tories) in Britain's long history. That was a major achievement in and of itself, since for centuries British politics had been essentially an "old boys' club" that viewed running a country as men's work. If rising to such a high position in a powerful nation, despite the social and other limitations placed on her gender, had been her most notable accomplishment, it would have been an impressive enough legacy. However, Thatcher managed much more. She went on to win election as the nation's first woman prime minister. And she won two more elections, making her the first British prime minister in over 150 years to win three consecutive terms, as well as the longest-serving head of state in modern British history, surpassing even the legendary Winston Churchill.

It would be natural to assume that such remarkable political success was the result of Thatcher's widespread popularity among the British. But such an assumption would be inaccurate if one defines popularity in the broad sense, as being "liked" as a person. As her eminent biographer, Hugo Young, points out:

> Little evidence could ever be produced that many people liked her, still less loved her. For her part, she did not seem to like them. . . . Although a populist [a champion of the common people], she was the ultimate argument against the contention that a political leader needs, in her person, to be popular.[93]

What made people vote for and support Thatcher, Young suggests, were two qualities: first, her image as a strong and moral person who refused to waver in her beliefs; and second, her innate ability to sense what the people wanted from her as a leader. "The determination to pursue the economics of sound housekeeping," says Young, which she

> elevated above the merely political to the moral level, came from within her. . . . She [also] had to a fine degree the political leader's sense of what would play well with the voters, and, very often, where to compromise . . . in order to secure the greater good. She was a consummate populist. Whether on union reform, or the nuclear bomb . . . or censorship . . . or attitudes to money, she invariably touched the majority nerve.[94]

Thatcher hit this nerve most forcibly when she directed the nation's military forces in a short but important war with Argentina, a venture overwhelmingly approved by the British public. In short, she was in many ways, regardless of her gender, the right person at the right time for Britain.

Her Father's Teachings

Margaret Thatcher later credited her father, Alfred Roberts, with imparting to her the ideas and worldview that made her a natural and successful politician and leader. Roberts and his wife, Beatrice, ran a small grocery store in Grantham, a market town in Lincolnshire, a rural section of east-central England. Thatcher, born Margaret Hilda Roberts on October 13, 1925, grew up in the family's quarters above the store. "My father's background as a grocer is sometimes cited as the basis for my economic philosophy," she later recalled.

> So it was—and is—but his original philosophy encompassed more than simply ensuring that incomings [income] showed a small surplus over outgoings [expenses] at the end of the week. My father . . . liked to connect the progress of our corner shop with the great complex romance of international trade which recruited people all over the world to ensure that a family in Grantham could have on its table rice from India, coffee from Kenya [in Africa], sugar from the West Indies and spices from five continents. I knew from my father's accounts that the free market was like a vast sensitive nervous system, responding to events and signals all over the world to meet the ever-changing needs of peoples in different countries. . . . The economic history of Britain for the next forty years

confirmed and amplified almost every item of my father's practical economics. In effect, I had been equipped at an early age with the ideal mental outlook and tools of analysis for reconstructing [a national economy].[95]

However valuable her father's teachings, as a youngster growing up in the 1930s and 1940s Margaret Thatcher did not in the least envision that she would ever wield national power and influence. In fact, for a long time she never even seriously considered a career in politics. It was rare for young women to do so, partly because the field was almost completely dominated by men; as late as 1952, when Thatcher was twenty-seven, only 17 of the country's 624 MPs (members of Parliament) were women. Moreover, society still routinely channeled most women into the traditional female roles and jobs, including wife, mother, grade-school teacher, secretary, and seamstress. Combining marriage and motherhood with a career was seen as difficult or inappropriate and often discouraged.

Balancing Motherhood and a Career

Yet Thatcher was one of the minority of headstrong women who broke free of tradition, set difficult, challenging goals for themselves, and successfully balanced raising a family with full-time work. An excellent student, she set her sights on Oxford University, one of the most prestigious universities in the world, ignoring her high school principal's warning that she was "overreaching her station" in life. Accepted at Oxford in 1943, the young woman majored in chemistry, a field dominated by men. She also joined Oxford's Conservative Association, a student group that studied and debated politics and nurtured future politicians. Eventually she rose through the group's ranks to the position of president, a highly unusual feat for a woman. Politics became her first love and not long after graduating from Oxford she began attending Tory political meetings and seriously considering a career in government.

It was at one of these political meetings that she met and fell in love with a businessman named Denis Thatcher. They married in December 1951 and the following year she gave birth to twins, whom they named Mark and Carol. These events marked an important juncture in Margaret Thatcher's life. Should she, like the vast majority of women in those days, become a full-time and permanent mother and housewife? Her answer was no and she gave the following rationale:

On her silver wedding anniversary (December 13, 1976), Margaret Thatcher poses with her husband, Denis, and children, Mark and Carol.

Why have so few women in recent years risen to the top of their professions? One reason may be that so many have cut short their careers when they marry. *In my view this is a great pity.* For it *is* possible to carry on working, taking a short leave of absence when families arrive, and returning later. In this way gifts and talents that would otherwise be wasted are developed to the benefit of the community.[96]

If this statement seems obvious today, when so many millions of women successfully combine raising families and working, it was decidedly unusual and controversial when Thatcher made it in 1952.

Conservative Principles and Virtues

Indeed, in the years that followed, Thatcher proved herself an excellent mother while managing to establish herself in the fast-paced and competitive realm of national politics. She won her first election to the House of Commons (Parliament's principal and most powerful branch) in 1959, representing Finchley, a small suburb of London. Part of a nationwide Tory landslide, she garnered 29,697 votes, as compared to her nearest opponent's 13,437 votes. Her constituents in Finchley, as well as her colleagues in the House, were impressed by her seemingly boundless energy, no-nonsense approach to her job, and unswerving dedication to her principles. These principles were conservative across the board. She extolled the virtues of freedom, hard work, thrift, and personal responsibility; she also staunchly advocated reducing the size of government, lowering taxes, cutting back welfare programs, encouraging free enterprise, restricting the powers of trade unions, and maintaining a strong military. Thatcher articulated and fought for these principles so effectively that she steadily rose through the Conservative ranks and by 1975 had become leader of the party, the first woman ever in that role.

This put Thatcher in a unique position. At the time, the rival Labor Party was in power and the Conservatives were the "opposition" party in the House. Sooner or later, the Conservatives would challenge Labor for control of the legislature, raising the possibility that Thatcher, a woman, might become prime minister. Popular discontent with the way Labor was running the country eventually transformed this possibility into reality. By the end of 1978 it was clear that the ruling Labor government was in trouble. Unemployment was high (over 1.3 million workers could not find jobs) and the country's economy had weakened to the point that Britain had earned the unflattering nickname of "the Sick Man of Europe." Moreover, polls showed that 89 percent of the British believed that trade unions, which had organized large, disruptive strikes in 1978, had amassed excessive power. More people than ever agreed with Thatcher that the unions needed to be regulated, while the Labor Party remained closely associated with the increasingly unpopular unions.

The volatile political atmosphere exploded in March 1979 when Thatcher, who by now had earned her own nickname, "the Iron Lady," [97] called for a vote of "no confidence" in the House. If enough MPs voted against the ruling Labor government, it would have to resign and a new election would have to be held. The vote

80

was 311 to 310 against the Labor Party. Realizing that Thatcher had forced the prime minister and his cabinet out of office, an event that had not occurred in Britain since 1924, Conservative MPs raised a cheer in the House chamber. They raised an even bigger cheer, along with millions of other citizens, when Thatcher won the ensuing election (in May), becoming the nation's first female prime minister.

The Falklands Factor

The cheers died away rather quickly, however. Thatcher cut both interest rates and public spending in an effort to curb inflation and thereby stimulate economic growth. But Britain's economic situation continued to worsen rather than improve. Between 1979 and 1981, unemployment continued to rise and a record number of ten thousand businesses went bankrupt, sending Thatcher's public approval rating down to a dismal 28 percent. Many financial experts, including several from her own party, urged her to turn away from her policies and try another approach. But she insisted on staying the course and giving these policies time to work. "This lady's not for turning," [98] she declared firmly (a takeoff on the title of a famous English play, Christopher Fry's *The Lady's Not for Burning*). Popular discontent became so great that it began to look as if the new prime minister might herself be toppled by a no-confidence vote.

Then, all at once, everything changed, both for Margaret Thatcher and Britain. On April 2, 1982, Argentina invaded and occupied the Falkland Islands. Lying in the Atlantic Ocean off the

Margaret Thatcher (seated at left) attends a Conservative Party meeting in the 1960s. She later became party leader and prime minister.

eastern coast of South America, the Falklands had been a British territory since 1833. But the Argentines had claimed sovereignty over the islands all along; and now they resorted to force to assert that claim. Argentine leaders gambled that the British, who had obvious financial difficulties, would not waste precious resources trying to win back a handful of tiny, distant islands inhabited by only a few thousand people. But they gambled wrong. Thatcher argued that the Falkland islanders were British subjects who wanted to remain so. Furthermore, as she later put it:

> What we were fighting for eight thousand miles away in the South Atlantic was not only the territory and the people of the Falklands, important though they were. We were defending our honor as a nation, and principles of fundamental importance to the whole world—above all that aggressors should never succeed and that international law should prevail over the use of force.[99]

The vast majority of British citizens, including most of Thatcher's colleagues in Parliament, strongly agreed with her tough, patriotic stance and supported her call for the use of force to get the islands back. A cartoon in the *Daily Express* showed her

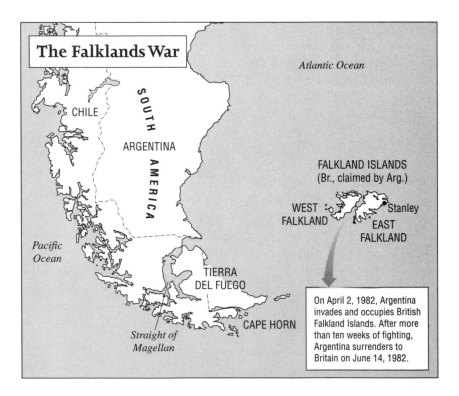

The Falklands War

Atlantic Ocean

CHILE

SOUTH AMERICA

ARGENTINA

FALKLAND ISLANDS
(Br., claimed by Arg.)

WEST FALKLAND

Stanley

EAST FALKLAND

Pacific Ocean

TIERRA DEL FUEGO

CAPE HORN

Straight of Magellan

On April 2, 1982, Argentina invades and occupies British Falkland Islands. After more than ten weeks of fighting, Argentina surrenders to Britain on June 14, 1982.

clad as Boudicca, the first-century British queen who had defended her people against the Romans, with metal breastplate and upraised sword. As she sent nearly a hundred warships and troop transports southward, her approval rating jumped to 83 percent. The Falklands War lasted just over ten weeks. Their bluff having been called and facing one of the world's strongest nations, the Argentines had no chance of winning and surrendered on June 14, 1982. Nonetheless, the fighting had been fierce, causing the deaths of some 650 Argentines and 250 British.

Happy about the victory, Thatcher declared that it had "put the Great back in Britain"[100] (referring to the fact that in recent decades Great Britain had acquired the image of a declining power). The victory, the political effects of which came to be called the "Falklands factor," had also restored confidence in Thatcher's Tory government. A majority of the British were now convinced that they had a strong, principled leader whose domestic policies should be given time to work. In 1983 Thatcher won her second election as prime minister by a landslide, enjoying the largest victory margin of any party since 1945. And, per her prediction, the economy did steadily and measurably improve under her leadership, contributing significantly to her third campaign victory in 1987.

The End of an Era

Margaret Thatcher led her nation so long, so vigorously, and with so much popular support that it came as a surprise to most people, both inside and outside Britain, when her tenure as prime minister ended suddenly in 1990. Over the course of that year, several of her most powerful colleagues in the Conservative Party came increasingly to disagree with her on important issues. This dissension eventually threatened to weaken the party and to keep her from governing effectively, so she resigned on November 22. Although the Conservatives remained in power, it was clearly the end of an era for Britain. In her farewell speech to Parliament, Thatcher defended the forceful posture she had taken, both in the Falklands crisis and on domestic issues. "When principles have to be defended," she said, "when good has to be upheld and when evil has to be overcome, Britain will take up arms. It is because we on this side [i.e., the Conservatives] have never flinched from difficult decisions that this . . . country can have confidence in this Government today."[101] Indeed, even those who disagreed with her politics and policies had to concede that, like her illustrious predecessor Boudicca, in the face of formidable odds Margaret Thatcher had never flinched.

CHAPTER 9

Benazir Bhutto: Daughter of Destiny

On December 1, 1988, a thirty-five-year-old woman named Benazir Bhutto became prime minister of the nation of Pakistan. This was unarguably one of the most extraordinary personal and political feats of the twentieth century; for she had come to power in a Muslim country in which men traditionally held almost all positions of authority and responsibility. In fact, Bhutto was the first woman to lead a Muslim nation in modern times.

Another factor that made Bhutto's election victory extraordinary was the horrendous personal ordeal she had endured to achieve it. Most people living outside of Pakistan and its immediate neighbors learned about her for the first time when she became prime minister. They heard news reports mentioning that she had undergone "a long struggle," but few realized the extent of that struggle. Over the course of more than a decade, Bhutto had courageously faced threats, imprisonment, exile, physical abuse, mental anguish, and the murder of family members and friends; yet she had managed to endure and ultimately to overcome all of these obstacles. Through it all, it had been the memory and inspiration of her father, Ali Bhutto, that had sustained her. "Stand up to challenge," she later wrote, summing up what she had learned from him.

> Fight against overwhelming odds. Overcome the enemy. In the stories my father had told us over and over as children, good always triumphed over evil. "Whether you grasp an opportunity or let it slip away, whether you are impetuous or thoughtful, whether you have unsinkable nerves or are timid, all of these choices are up to you," he had always impressed upon us. "What you make of your destinies is up to you." [102]

Ali Bhutto did not live to see his daughter fulfill a major part of her destiny by becoming prime minister. But the two causes she fought for most passionately—the dignity of women and democratic government—were his causes, too. She knew in her heart, therefore, the tremendous pride he would have felt in her achievement.

A Privileged Childhood

Benazir Bhutto's inspiring story began on June 21, 1953, when she was born into Ali Bhutto's household in Karachi, a large city on Pakistan's southern coast. The Bhutto family had long held considerable wealth and prestige, as well as the largest land holdings, in the local province of Sindh. "Our lands," Benazir would later write,

> were measured in square miles, not acres. As children we loved to hear the story of the amazement of Charles Napier, the British conqueror of Sindh in 1843. "Whose lands are these?" he repeatedly asked his driver as he toured the province. "Bhutto's lands," came the inevitable response. "Wake me up when we are off Bhutto's lands," he ordered. He was surprised when some time later he woke up on his own. "Who owns this land?" he asked. "Bhutto," the driver repeated.[103]

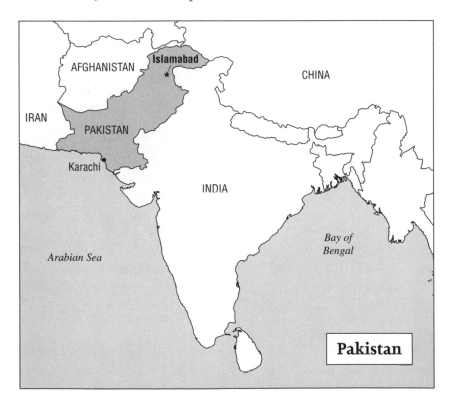

Later, Benazir's grandfather, Shah Nawaz Bhutto, had been knighted by the British, who then controlled India (Pakistan had not yet separated from India).[104] Sir Shah Nawaz was a highly enlightened man who believed that all children, including young girls, should be well educated, a progressive attitude in his society at the time. "He educated his children," the grown-up Benazir recalled,

> even sending his daughters to school, an act that was considered scandalous by the other landowners. Many feudals [powerful landowners] did not even bother to educate their sons. "My sons have land. They have a guaranteed income, and will never . . . work for anyone else. My daughters will inherit land, and be looked after by their husbands or their brothers. So why bother with education?" ran the feudal ethos [belief system].[105]

Thus, Ali Bhutto, Sir Shah Nawaz's son, studied in both the United States and Britain and came to be even more socially and politically enlightened than his father. In 1951, four years after the British had relinquished control of India, which then separated into two countries, India and Pakistan, Ali married Nusrat, the daughter of a wealthy Iranian businessman. Nusrat and her daughters, Benazir and Sanam, did not have to live in separate women's quarters, then the common custom. Nor did Benazir have to wear the *burqa*, the black veils that most Muslim women were expected to put on when leaving their quarters or appearing before strangers. Instead, Benazir enjoyed the luxury of wearing the *shalwar khameez,* Pakistan's national dress, consisting of baggy trousers and a long tunic.

Pakistani prime minister Ali Bhutto answers news reporters' questions during a press conference on an official visit to Paris.

Benazir enjoyed other luxuries and privileges as well. Over twenty servants looked after the family's house and grounds. And Ali, who wanted to improve the status of Pakistani women, made sure that Benazir (along with his other children, Sanam and two sons, Mir and Shah) received the best education possible. In 1969, at age sixteen, Benazir began her studies at Radcliffe College, which later became part of the prestigious Harvard University, in the United States. There, the young woman saw firsthand how free, educated, and socially mobile Western women were in comparison to most women in her homeland. This made her as determined as her father to improve the status of female Pakistanis.

The Long Ordeal

During her tenure at Radcliffe, Benazir was distressed to learn that her native land had become wracked by war and civil strife. The western and eastern sectors of Pakistan clashed over economic and political differences; in 1971 eastern Pakistan declared itself independent and became the nation of Bangladesh. Ali Bhutto, by now a figure of national reputation, became president of the remaining, western section of Pakistan, which was a democracy with a government modeled on the British parliamentary system.

In the next few years, Benazir continued her education while her father governed Pakistan. Whenever she had school vacations and breaks, he took her along with him on visits to foreign nations. This is how she met Mao Tse-tung, the leader of Communist China, and U.S. president Richard Nixon. When she graduated with honors from Radcliffe in 1973, Benazir went on to study international affairs at Oxford University. Meanwhile, Ali and his party, the Peoples Party of Pakistan (PPP), won the new elections held early in 1977.

Unfortunately for the Bhutto family, its good fortunes were soon transformed into tragedy. Not long after the 1977 election, it became clear that the Pakistani military, headed by General Muhammed Zia ul-Haq, was uneasy about civilians holding so much power. President Bhutto also faced opposition from rich land and factory owners who thought his policies were too progressive. On July 5, 1977, sensing Bhutto's power base weakening, General Zia seized power. Claiming that the PPP had rigged the recent election (a charge later proved false), the army leader suspended the constitution, outlawed all political parties, and arrested the members of the Bhutto family, including Benazir. Moreover, Zia, a strict Muslim who disliked the Bhuttos' modern ideas about traditional religious and social customs, instituted an era of religious repression. According to Benazir Bhutto:

> To further intimidate the people, Zia unleashed the forces
> of the religious fundamentalists. Whether or not to fast

during the holy month of Ramadan had always been the personal choice of Muslims in Pakistan. Under Zia, public restaurants and food concessions were ordered closed from sunup to sundown. At the universities, water was shut off in the campus water fountains and even in the bathrooms to prevent anyone from taking a drink during the fast. Fundamentalist gangs freely roamed the streets, banging on doors in the middle of the night to make sure people were preparing *sehri,* the predawn meal. Smoking cigarettes, drinking water, or eating in public was punishable by arrest. There was to be no more personal choice in Pakistan, only the strong arm of the supposedly religious regime.[106]

Muhammed Zia ul-Haq, the military strongman who drove Ali Bhutto from power and installed himself as dictator.

The religious crackdown and imposition of martial law marked only the beginning of a long ordeal for Pakistan and the Bhutto family. Zia put Ali Bhutto on trial, unjustly sentenced him to death, and, ignoring pleas from hundreds of world leaders and organizations to pardon him, executed Ali in April 1979. Benazir and her mother were terrorized and repeatedly arrested and imprisoned (Mir and Shah were already in exile by this time). At one point Benazir was confined in a filthy, insect-infested cell. The cell was so hot and her diet so poor that boils erupted on her face, her hair began to fall out, and infections wracked her body. The one doctor who came to treat her punctured her eardrum (either out of incompetence or on Zia's orders), causing her to go deaf in one ear. Meanwhile, the government arrested anyone who sympathized with the Bhuttos or expressed a desire for the nation to return to democracy; by 1981 there were over forty thousand political prisoners in Pakistani jails.

A Trip to the United States

Eventually Benazir and her mother were allowed to leave the country. Apparently Zia believed he had broken them and that the Bhuttos were no longer a threat to his dictatorship. But he was sorely mistaken. Benazir went first to Switzerland and then to London, where she became both a symbolic and real leader of exiled PPP members who longed to overthrow Zia and restore democracy in their country. In 1984 Benazir flew to the United States. There she lobbied senators and other leaders, urging them to stop supporting Zia. (Despite Zia's record of civil rights abuses, President Ronald Reagan's administration had backed and funded him in order to give the United States a base of operations for supporting the Afghan rebels then fighting the Soviet Union.) While in Washington, D.C., Benazir published a magazine titled *Amal (Action)*, which told the truth about what was happening in Pakistan.

A Sea of Humanity

These and other tireless efforts, in which Benazir fully utilized all of the courage, political skills, and important personal contacts she had inherited from her father, eventually began to pay off. Under U.S. pressure, in December 1985 Zia was forced to lift martial law in Pakistan. Then Benazir stunned world leaders, not to mention Zia and her compatriots, by announcing that, regardless of the potential dangers, she would return to Pakistan, defy the dictator, and fight for democracy.[107] When her plane landed on April 10, 1986, at Lahore, a large city in the northeastern part of the country, gigantic crowds enthusiastically greeted her. "There are moments in life which are not possible to describe," she recorded later in her autobiography, *Daughter of Destiny*.

> My return to Lahore was one of them. The sea of humanity lining the roads, jammed on balconies and roofs, wedged in trees and on lampposts . . . and stretching back across the fields, was more like an ocean. The eight-mile drive from the airport to [downtown Lahore] usually takes fifteen minutes. On the unbelievable day of April 10, 1986, it took us ten hours. The figure of one million people at the airport grew to two million, then three million.[108]

Benazir went on to tour the country, where thousands of jubilant Pakistanis continued to cheer her. Zia attempted, through more crackdowns and arrests, to stop the political tidal wave she had sent sweeping across the land, but his efforts were in vain. On August 17, 1988, he died in a plane crash and a former Pakistani senator named Ghulam Ishaq Khan quickly took temporary charge of the government, restoring civilian rule. Khan called for new elections. These were held on November 17, and the PPP, now headed by Benazir Bhutto, won. When party leaders chose her as prime minister on December 1, she became, at age thirty-five, after an incredible struggle, the first woman ever to hold such high office in Pakistan.

The Conscience of the Country

Benazir wasted no time in restoring full democracy to her nation. She immediately pardoned and released all political prisoners and reinstated full freedom of the press. Yet such reforms, though important, could not undo overnight the many wrongs the dictatorship had perpetrated, nor could they quickly solve the nation's numerous pressing problems. Over 70 percent of Pakistanis were still illiterate. The former parliamentary and legal systems had been dismantled for so long that there remained few trained legislators and judges. Bribery and smuggling had become widespread, and armed bandits routinely robbed stores and held families hostage for ransom. Perhaps worst of all, the vast majority of people remained, as they had been for centuries, trapped in crushing poverty.

Benazir Bhutto lost the prime ministership of Pakistan in 1990 but regained it in 1993.

Though Prime Minister Bhutto worked relentlessly to alleviate these problems, they were too engrained and widespread to solve in only one or two years. Yet the Pakistani people wanted, and naively expected, quick results. So many were disappointed with the new PPP government that they came to believe leaders of opposition parties when they accused it of corruption. In August 1990 the nation's president dismissed the Bhutto regime and called for new elections, which the PPP lost.[109]

Bhutto refused to stay beaten. The new leaders soon displayed the same difficulties she had in reforming the country and the PPP, now the opposition party, took its turn criticizing government policies. In 1993, amid serious constitutional and other disputes, both the president and the prime minister resigned, paving the way for new elections that put Bhutto back in power. This time, however, she did not receive a mandate from her compatriots. The PPP held eighty-six seats in the national legislature, only slightly more than the seventy-two seats held by the opposition party. The next three years witnessed continued political unrest and religious fighting, as terrorists attempted to overthrow the government and establish a fundamentalist Islamic state. In November 1996 Bhutto was dismissed once more, again on charges of corruption. (As of early 1998, no evidence has been found supporting these charges.)

Since her second dismissal, Benazir Bhutto has remained a loud and influential voice in Pakistani affairs; and she never shrinks from condemning any governmental policy or action she deems detrimental to the nation's democratic or national interests. In May 1998, for example, she roundly criticized her former opponent, Prime Minister Nawaz Sharif. The weakness of his regime, she claimed, had prompted Pakistan's neighbor and rival, India, to test five nuclear devices in an effort to intimidate Pakistan.

Whether critics agree or disagree with her opinions and politics, few have any doubt that Benazir Bhutto will continue to speak out. Ever righteous and optimistic, she believes that the party her father created is the true voice of her people. "We were, and are, the conscience of the country," she has said, "the future and the hope. Our day, I know, will come." [110]

NOTES

Introduction: "Singular Exceptions" in a Man's World

1. *Chronicles of Castile's Rulers,* quoted in Peggy K. Liss, *Isabel the Queen: Life and Times.* New York: Oxford University Press, 1992, p. 1.
2. *First Blast of the Trumpet Against the Monstrous Regiment of Women,* quoted in Will Durant, *The Reformation.* New York: Simon and Schuster, 1957, p. 612.
3. Vicki Leon, *Uppity Women of Medieval Times.* Berkeley, CA: Conari Press, 1997, p. XII.
4. Quoted in Lucy Hughes-Hallet, *Cleopatra: Histories, Dreams, and Distortions.* New York: HarperCollins, 1991, p. 1.
5. Edward Gibbon, *The Decline and Fall of the Roman Empire.* Vol. 1, ed. David Womersley. New York: Penguin Books, 1994, p. 170.

Chapter 1: Warrior Women Through the Ages

6. The *Amazonomachy* was depicted in the bas-reliefs on the Doric frieze (the band of sculptures running horizontally above the columns) on the building's west end. A battle with Amazons was also carved (or possibly painted) onto the outside surface of the shield held by the huge statue of Athena that stood inside the temple. The victory of Greeks over Amazons was seen as a manifestation of civilization triumphing over barbarism.
7. Herodotus, *The Histories,* trans. Aubrey de Sélincourt. New York: Penguin Books, 1972, p. 308.
8. "Warrior Women of the Eurasian Steppes," *Archaeology,* January/February 1997, pp. 47–48.
9. Herodotus, *The Histories,* p. 115.
10. Herodotus, *The Histories,* p. 127. Herodotus's description of the confrontation between Cyrus and Tomyris (see pp. 123–28) is fulsome, colorful, and well worth reading in its entirety. In his extensive travels, he visited Persia, where he likely heard detailed and fairly reliable reports about Tomyris, who had lived and died only a few decades before.
11. Quoted in Herodotus, *The Histories,* p. 553.
12. Colin Wells, *The Roman Empire.* London: Fontana, 1992, p. 271.

13. Quoted in Dio Cassius, *Roman History,* excerpted in *The Roman History: The Reign of Augustus,* trans. Ian Scott-Kilvert. New York: Penguin Books, 1987, pp. 52–53.

14. Antonia Fraser, *The Warrior Queens: The Legends and the Lives of the Women Who Have Led Their Nations in War.* New York: Random House, 1988, pp. 17–18.

15. This was a common custom among Rome's subservient client-rulers, a kind of bribe with which such a ruler intended to placate the Romans and ensure their kind treatment of his heirs.

16. Tacitus, *Annals,* trans. Michael Grant. New York: Penguin Books, 1989, p. 328.

17. Tacitus, *Annals,* pp. 330–31. Tacitus's mention of the natives' wagons refers to the common practice among ancient Celtic tribal warriors of keeping their wives, children, and belongings nearby during battle. Needless to say, over the centuries this custom led to the slaughter of hundreds of thousands of innocent noncombatants.

18. Fraser, *The Warrior Queens,* p. 109.

19. Gibbon, *Decline and Fall,* vol. 1, p. 313.

20. Gibbon, *Decline and Fall,* vol. 1, p. 313.

21. Quoted in Will Durant, *The Age of Faith.* New York: Simon and Schuster, 1950, pp. 549–50.

22. Among other distinguished scholars, she invited the renowned French philosopher René Descartes (1596–1650) to her court and learned much from him.

23. Fraser, *The Warrior Queens,* pp. 333–34.

24. Quoted in William Safire, ed., *Lend Me Your Ears: Great Speeches in History.* New York: W. W. Norton, 1997, pp. 566–67. Lady Astor was born Nancy Langhorne in the U.S. state of Virginia in 1879. She married Waldorf Astor, a member of Britain's House of Commons, who was elevated to the House of Lords in 1910. She subsequently won election to his old seat in the Commons. A tireless worker for women's rights, she retired from Parliament in 1945 and died in 1964.

Chapter 2: Cleopatra: A Woman for All Ages

25. *Life of Antony,* in *Makers of Rome: Nine Lives by Plutarch,* trans. Ian Scott-Kilvert. New York: Penguin Books, 1965, pp. 292–93.

26. The Greeks called their homeland Hellas and themselves Hellenes; therefore, the term *Hellenic* means Greek. Because the

kingdoms established by Alexander's generals featured various mergers of Greek and Near Eastern cultures, historians call them Hellenistic, or "Greek-like," the name also given to the age lasting from Alexander's death in 323 B.C. to Cleopatra's demise in 31 B.C.

27. Naphtali Lewis, *Life in Egypt Under Roman Rule.* Oxford, England: Clarendon Press, 1983, p. 10.

28. Quoted in *War Commentaries of Caesar,* trans. Rex Warner. New York: New American Library, 1960, p. 328.

29. Quoted in *War Commentaries of Caesar,* p. 328.

30. *Life of Caesar,* in *Fall of the Roman Republic: Six Lives by Plutarch,* trans. Rex Warner. New York: Penguin Books, 1972, p. 290.

31. "Up" because, although they traveled away from the Mediterranean port of Alexandria and southward geographically speaking, the Egyptians referred to the portion of their land lying toward the Nile's source (south on a modern map) as "Upper Egypt" and the portion nearer the Mediterranean (north on a modern map) as "Lower Egypt."

32. Quoted in *Julius Caesar,* in *Lives of the Twelve Caesars,* published as *The Twelve Caesars,* trans. Robert Graves, rev. Michael Grant. New York: Penguin Books, 1979, p. 36.

33. They had met at least twice, if briefly, years before. The first time was when he was a young officer in the Roman force that rescued Auletes' throne in 57 B.C. (when she was about twelve). The second was the interval during which she visited Rome just prior to Caesar's assassination in 44 B.C.

34. *Life of Antony,* in *Makers of Rome,* p. 293.

35. They had earlier pushed the weaker Lepidus aside, placing him under permanent house arrest.

36. Peter Green, *Alexander to Actium: The Historical Evolution of the Hellenistic Age.* Berkeley and Los Angeles: University of California Press, 1990, p. 682.

Chapter 3: Isabella: "The Traveling Queen"

37. Baldesar Castiglione, *The Book of the Courtier,* trans. Charles S. Singleton. New York: Doubleday, 1959, p. 237.

38. Nancy Rubin, *Isabella of Castile: The First Renaissance Queen.* New York: St. Martin's Press, 1991, p. 7.

39. Rubin, *Isabella of Castile,* p. 29.

40. Alonso de Palencia, *Chronicles of Enrique IV,* quoted in Rubin, *Isabella of Castile,* p. 83.

41. From the anonymous *Incomplete Chronicle,* quoted in Liss, *Isabel the Queen,* p. 117.

42. Ironically, the name Castile means "country of castles." Thus, in leveling these venerable old monuments, the monarchy, while making itself more powerful and secure, forever eradicated much of the land's rich ancient and medieval history.

43. Economic reforms included the following: the banning of private coin minting, making the royal coinage more standardized and valuable; the creation of standardized taxes on exports and imports; the abolition of tariffs on goods traded between Castile and Aragon; and the introduction of royal licensing for all major commercial ventures, which later allowed the crown to capitalize handsomely on discoveries made by Columbus and other explorers.

44. Andres de Bernaldez, *History of the Catholic Rulers,* quoted in Liss, *Isabel the Queen,* pp. 273–74.

45. Quoted in Rubin, *Isabella of Castile,* p. 462.

Chapter 4: Elizabeth I: England's Loving Mother

46. Quoted in Lacey B. Smith, *Elizabethan World.* New York: American Heritage, 1967, p. 335.

47. Elizabeth's legitimacy was never legally reestablished; however, a statute passed in 1554 regarding the royal succession ignored the issue and placed her third in line to the throne after Henry's other children, Edward (born in 1537) and Mary (born in 1516).

48. Many members were reluctant because they did not like being guided and lobbied by the monarchy, preferring to suggest and pass legislation on their own initiative and thereby in a sense to guide the crown; some were reluctant at first to follow a woman's advice and lead; and still others were Catholics (some of them bishops), who were solidly against the reinstatement of Protestantism.

49. Smith, *Elizabethan World,* p. 87.

50. Smith, *Elizabethan World,* p. 98.

51. Elizabeth Jenkins, *Elizabeth the Great.* New York: Coward-McCann, 1958, pp. 164–65.

52. From *The Fugger News-Letters,* quoted in Leon Bernard and Theodore B. Hodges, eds., *Readings in European History.* New York: Macmillan, 1958, p. 246.

53. Quoted in Catherine Bush, *Elizabeth I*. New York: Chelsea House, 1985, p. 89.

54. Quoted in Smith, *Elizabethan World*, p. 335.

55. Because she never married and had children (and because Henry VIII's other children had died before having children), the Tudor line was extinguished. The son of Mary, queen of Scots, James Stuart, a Protestant, succeeded Elizabeth as England's next monarch.

56. Katherine Anthony, *Queen Elizabeth*. New York: Knopf, 1929, p. 258.

Chapter 5: Catherine the Great: An Iron Will and a Restless Heart

57. Claude C. de Rulhiere, *A History of Anecdotes of the Revolution in Russia in the Year 1762,* quoted in John T. Alexander, *Catherine the Great: Life and Legend*. New York: Oxford University Press, 1989, p. 5.

58. Nicholas V. Riasanovsky, *A History of Russia*. New York: Oxford University Press, 1984, p. 256.

59. The charge, leveled from time to time over the years, that she ordered or took part in his murder is probably false. The best evidence suggests that a group of army officers, acting in what they considered her and the country's best interests, carried out the assassination and informed her afterward.

60. De Rulhiere, *A History of Anecdotes,* quoted in Alexander, *Catherine the Great*, pp. 5–7.

61. John Perry, *The State of Russia Under the Present Czar,* quoted in Bernard and Hodges, eds., *Readings in European History,* pp. 299–301.

62. Quoted in Robert Coughlan, *Elizabeth and Catherine, Empresses of All the Russias*. New York: G. P. Putnam's Sons, 1974, p. 198.

63. Her first set of plays, begun in 1772, were comedies that good-naturedly poked fun at Russian life and manners; these inspired the playwright Denis Fonfizin to pen *The Minor,* the outstanding Russian play of the era. Catherine's second group of plays, begun in 1786, were comedies and historical dramas inspired by Shakespeare's works; thanks in large part to her efforts, Shakespeare's influence helped to shape the ensuing development of Russian drama.

64. Catherine II, *Memoirs,* trans. Moura Budberg, ed. Dominique Maroger. New York: Macmillan, 1961, p. 356.

65. Quoted in Coughlan, *Elizabeth and Catherine*, p. 322.

Chapter 6: Victoria: "The Grandmother of Europe"

66. Quoted in Helmut and Alison Gernsheim, *Victoria R.: A Biography with Four Hundred Illustrations Based on Her Personal Photograph Albums*. New York: G. P. Putnam's Sons, 1959, p. 7.
67. "The Liberal Age (1851–1914)," in Kenneth O. Morgan, ed., *The Oxford Illustrated History of Britain*. New York: Oxford University Press, 1986, pp. 494–96.
68. Quoted in Gernsheim, *Victoria R.*, pp. 7–8.
69. Quoted in Stanley Weintraub, *Victoria: An Intimate Biography*. New York: E. P. Dutton, 1987, p. 123.
70. Quoted in Gernsheim, *Victoria R.*, p. 14.
71. Quoted in Gernsheim, *Victoria R.*, p. 39.
72. Among Victoria's and Albert's illustrious grandchildren were William II, Kaiser of Germany during World War I, and Alexandra, queen consort of Russia's Czar Nicholas II, who lost his throne during the Russian Revolution. In all, thirty-seven of Victoria's grandchildren survived her.
73. Quoted in Gernsheim, *Victoria R.*, p. 52.
74. Quoted in Gernsheim, *Victoria R.*, p. 140.
75. Quoted in Weintraub, *Victoria*, p. 374.
76. Quoted in Weintraub, *Victoria*, p. 390. An excellent film reenactment of their relationship and the ensuing scandal—*Her Majesty, Mrs. Brown*, starring the distinguished British actress Judi Dench as Victoria—appeared in 1997 and is available on video.
77. Quoted in Gernsheim, *Victoria R.*, p. 211.
78. Christopher Hibbert, *The Story of England*. London: Phaidon, 1992, p. 168.
79. Quoted in Christopher Hibbert, *Daily Life in Victorian England*. New York: American Heritage, 1975, p. 123.

Chapter 7: Golda Meir: The Woman Who Made Israel Possible

80. Ralph G. Martin, *Golda Meir: The Romantic Years*. New York: Scribner's, 1988, p. x.
81. Golda Meir, *My Life*. New York: G. P. Putnam's Sons, 1975, pp. 27–28.

82. Ancient Israel had divided into two states in the early first millennium B.C.; later, the Assyrians and the Babylonians conquered and absorbed these states. Palestine came under Roman rule in the last years of the first millennium B.C., and the Jews, who still maintained a temple in Jerusalem, frequently fought for their independence. In A.D. 70, however, the Romans sacked and devastated Jerusalem, burned the temple, and in subsequent centuries most Jews scattered to other lands, where they usually had to live in ghettos and endure cruel prejudice and brutality.

83. Meir, *My Life,* pp. 15–16.

84. Quoted in Martin, *Golda Meir,* p. 79. The statement was originally contained in a letter from Balfour to another British statesman and subsequently made public. Its wording was incorporated into the 1922 League of Nations Mandate for Palestine, although its promise was not fulfilled for nearly three more decades.

85. Meir, *My Life, p.* 58.

86. Quoted in Meir, *My Life,* pp. 212–13.

87. Quoted in Karen McAuley, *Golda Meir.* New York: Chelsea House, 1985, p. 63.

88. Quoted in Meir, *My Life,* p. 226.

89. Meir, *My Life,* p. 226.

90. Quoted in Martin, *Golda Meir,* p. 293.

91. Quoted in Martin, *Golda Meir,* p. 342.

92. Meir, *My Life,* pp. 460–61.

Chapter 8: Margaret Thatcher: Great Britain's Iron Lady

93. Hugo Young, *The Iron Lady.* New York: Farrar, Straus, Giroux, 1989, p. 545.

94. Young, *The Iron Lady,* pp. 544–45.

95. Margaret Thatcher, *The Downing Street Years.* New York: HarperCollins, 1993, p. 11.

96. Quoted in George Gardiner, *Margaret Thatcher: From Childhood to Leadership.* London: William Kimber, 1975, p. 50.

97. Soviet leaders had given her the name, intending it in the derogatory sense, after she had given a series of speeches labeling the Communist Soviet Union as a threat to world peace and freedom. The name subsequently caught on in the West, where she smilingly used it herself on occasion.

98. Quoted in Penny Junor, *Margaret Thatcher: Wife, Mother, Politician.* London: Sidgwick, 1983, p. 153.

99. Thatcher, *The Downing Street Years,* p. 173.

100. Quoted in Bernard Garfinkel, *Margaret Thatcher.* New York: Chelsea House, 1985, p. 97.

101. Thatcher, *The Downing Street Years,* pp. 859–60.

Chapter 9: Benazir Bhutto: Daughter of Destiny

102. Benazir Bhutto, *Daughter of Destiny.* New York: Simon and Schuster, 1989, p. 30.

103. Bhutto, *Daughter of Destiny,* p. 39.

104. By the mid-1800s, the powerful British East India Company, which had begun exploiting India's land and people in the preceding century, controlled about three-fifths of the region. In 1858 the British government took over this control and expanded it, administering India until 1947, when the country gained its independence. At the time, the region was partitioned into two nations—largely Hindu India and largely Muslim Pakistan.

105. Bhutto, *Daughter of Destiny,* p. 41.

106. Bhutto, *Daughter of Destiny,* p. 107.

107. These dangers were very real. Shortly before she returned, a former family servant phoned her to warn that Zia's agents planned to assassinate her if she came back to Pakistan. Soon afterward, these agents murdered the man for warning her.

108. Bhutto, *Daughter of Destiny,* p. 326.

109. Pakistan practices a form of parliamentary democracy in which voters elect a president at the same time that they choose a political party to head a new government. The president, whose office acts as a check on the legislature and prime minister, has the legal right, in certain circumstances, to dismiss the ruling prime minister and his or her cabinet and to institute new elections.

110. Bhutto, *Daughter of Destiny,* p. 373.

CHRONOLOGY

B.C.

ca. 9th Century

Queen Sammuramat, whom the Greeks and Romans later called Semiramis, rules the mighty Assyrian Empire, centered in what is now Iraq, for five years while waiting for her son to come of age.

480

Artemisia, queen of the Greek kingdom of Caria (in Asia Minor), leads her ships and troops in the great sea battle of Salamis.

ca. 450

While traveling through the steppes near the Black Sea, the Greek historian Herodotus, later called "the Father of History," hears tales about the Amazons, a race of warrior women that supposedly invaded Athens long before.

69

Cleopatra VII, a princess of the Greek Ptolemaic family, then ruling Egypt, is born. In the same year, Julius Caesar, whose later relationship with her will make her famous, is rising through the ranks of Rome's political offices.

41

Three years after Caesar, her lover and ally and the father of her son, is assassinated, Cleopatra becomes lover and ally to Caesar's former assistant, Mark Antony. Antony and Cleopatra soon challenge Rome's might in an attempt to gain control of the Mediterranean world.

31

Cleopatra and Antony are decisively defeated at Actium in western Greece. They flee to Egypt and there take their own lives.

A.D.

60

Boudicca, queen of the Iceni, a Celtic tribe of south-central Britain, leads a widespread rebellion against the Romans. More than seventy thousand Romans are killed before Boudicca is defeated.

267

Zenobia, queen of the Syrian kingdom of Palmyra, succeeds her husband as sole ruler and, following the inspiration of Cleopatra and Boudicca, challenges Rome. After conquering Egypt and other Near Eastern regions, Zenobia is defeated by the Romans but goes on to create a new life for herself in Italy.

1076

Matilda, known as "the Grand Countess," inherits the vast lands of the Italian House of Canossa. Eight years later she leads her troops to victory over the armies of male foes attempting to usurp her realm.

1451

Isabella, princess and future queen of the Spanish kingdom of Castile, is born.

1469

Isabella marries Ferdinand, heir apparent to the throne of the neighboring kingdom of Aragon, marking the beginning of their unification of several Spanish kingdoms into a powerful nation.

1492

Isabella and Ferdinand sign an edict expelling Spanish Jews from the country and complete the conquest of the Moorish kingdom of Granada, on Spain's southern coast; having received Isabella's backing, the Italian navigator Christopher Columbus sets sail on his initial voyage to the New World.

1553–1558

Reign of England's Queen Mary, daughter of Henry VIII, who attempts to restore Catholicism to her country.

1558

Mary dies and her half sister, Elizabeth I, takes the throne; in the following year, Elizabeth enacts the "Elizabethan Settlement," ensuring that the nation will remain Protestant.

1588

Elizabeth's forces defeat the Spanish Armada, a huge fleet sent by Spain's king to depose her and restore Catholicism.

1603

Elizabeth dies, marking the end of the so-called Elizabethan Age, in which England enjoyed a cultural renaissance that included the works of William Shakespeare, Ben Jonson, and Christopher Marlowe.

1632

Princess Christina becomes queen of Sweden. In 1654, she abdicates her throne after secretly converting to Catholicism, a faith forbidden in her land.

1762

An obscure German princess ascends the Russian throne as Catherine II.

1768–1774

Catherine's forces battle the Turks in an attempt to acquire warm-water ports on the Black Sea.

1785

Catherine helps to maintain her power by granting the Russian aristocracy numerous rights and privileges.

1837

Princess Victoria ascends the English throne, marking the beginning of a long reign that will come to be called the Victorian Age in her honor.

1840

Victoria marries her first cousin, Albert, a German aristocrat, whose straitlaced attitudes and habits help to define the period's conservative image.

1851

Victoria's reign reaches its zenith in the Great Exhibition, a world's fair celebrating the advances of the Industrial Revolution and exemplifying British power and prosperity.

1898

Golda Mabovitch, later Golda Meir, who will later help found the modern state of Israel, is born into a poor Jewish family in the Russian Ukraine.

1901

Queen Victoria dies.

1921

Golda Meir moves to Palestine, where for decades she works unceasingly for the establishment of a Jewish homeland.

1948

Golda Meir raises $50 million to help facilitate the creation of Israel, which occurs on May 14 of that year.

1953

Benazir Bhutto, daughter of the progressive Pakistani landowner and politician, Ali Bhutto, is born.

1959

At age thirty-four, Margaret Thatcher wins her first election as a member of Britain's Parliament.

1969

Golda Meir becomes Israel's first woman prime minister; Benazir Bhutto begins attending Radcliffe College in the United States.

1975

Margaret Thatcher becomes head of Britain's Conservative Party, the first woman ever to head a major British political party; four years later she is elected as the nation's first female prime minister.

1979

Ali Bhutto, who had won two democratic elections in Pakistan, is executed by dictator Muhammed Zia ul-Haq; Benazir Bhutto begins a long ordeal of imprisonment, exile, and attempts to restore democracy in her country.

1982

When Argentina invades the Falkland Islands, a British territory in the South Atlantic, Margaret Thatcher mounts a massive military expedition that succeeds in restoring the islands to British control.

1986

After several years in exile, Benazir Bhutto returns in triumph to Pakistan and defies Zia; two years later she becomes prime minister, the first woman leader of a modern Muslim nation.

ca. 1990s

Archaeologists discover female graves containing weapons in the Russian steppes, suggesting that the ancient tales of the Amazons may have had a basis in fact.

FOR FURTHER READING

Author's Note: Each of the following volumes effectively chronicles the major events and issues of the life and times of the woman leader named in the title. All have formats and reading levels geared specifically to junior high and high school readers.

Katherine M. Doherty and Craig A. Doherty, *Benazir Bhutto.* New York: Franklin Watts, 1990.

Leila M. Foster, *Margaret Thatcher: First Woman Prime Minister of Great Britain.* Chicago: Childrens Press, 1990.

Deborah Hitzeroth, *Golda Meir.* San Diego: Lucent Books, 1997.

William W. Lace, *Elizabethan England.* San Diego: Lucent Books, 1995.

Leslie McGuire, *Catherine the Great.* New York: Chelsea House, 1986.

Don Nardo, *Cleopatra.* San Diego: Lucent Books, 1994.

Patricia Netzley, *Queen Victoria.* San Diego: Lucent Books, 1996.

Paul Stevens, *Ferdinand and Isabella.* New York: Chelsea House, 1988.

John T. Alexander, *Catherine the Great: Life and Legend*. New York: Oxford University Press, 1989. A commendable, up-to-date study of the Russian queen known variously as a political genius, a foreign usurper and adventuress, and an unusually prodigious lover. Also see Ian Grey, *Catherine the Great: Autocrat and Empress of All Russia*. Philadelpia: J. B. Lippincott, 1962.

Benazir Bhutto, *Daughter of Destiny*. New York: Simon and Schuster, 1989. The first woman to lead a Muslim nation in modern times tells her own story in this frank autobiography. Her father's brutal execution, her solitary confinement as a political prisoner, her dramatic return to Pakistan from political exile, and her extraordinary electoral mandate are all covered in detail.

Antonia Fraser, *The Warrior Queens: The Legends and the Lives of the Women Who Have Led Their Nations in War*. New York: Random House, 1988. This extremely well researched and documented volume examines the image of the "warrior queen" in history, using Boudicca (the first-century A.D. British queen who rebelled against the Romans) as a model of the archetype, and proceeding to detailed discussions of Zenobia, Matilda, Maud, Isabella, Elizabeth I, and other forceful women leaders. David E. Jones's *Women Warriors: A History* (Washington, DC: Brassey, 1997), another well-researched book, is similar in scope and intent but concentrates more on women who actually led troops or fought in battle. *Images of Women in Peace and War* (Madison: University of Wisconsin Press, 1987), by Sharon Macdonald et al., and *Women of Achievement* (New York: Harmony Books, 1981), by Alison Weir, are other worthwhile general studies of powerful, daring, or otherwise noteworthy women of history.

Helmut and Alison Gernsheim, *Victoria R.: A Biography with Four Hundred Illustrations Based on Her Personal Photograph Albums*. New York: G. P. Putnam's Sons, 1959. This unique biography of Victoria focuses heavily on her own point of view, as revealed by both her personal photos and much of her personal correspondence. A somewhat more comprehensive and more up-to-date study of Victoria is *Victoria: An Intimate Biography* (New York: E. P. Dutton, 1987), by Stanley Weintraub of Pennsylvania State University, an acknowledged authority on the Victorian era.

Lucy Hughes-Hallet, *Cleopatra: Histories, Dreams, and Distortions*. New York: HarperCollins, 1991. An extremely comprehensive study of Cleopatra, summarizing the known facts about her as well as exploring later interpretations and spin-offs of her legend. Jack Lindsay's *Cleopatra* (London: Constable, 1970) is also very well researched and worthwhile.

Elizabeth Jenkins, *Elizabeth the Great*. New York: Coward-McCann, 1958. A very thorough and well-written overview of the life and times of one of England's greatest and most colorful monarchs. Excellent supplements include Lacey B. Smith's *Elizabethan World* (New York: American Heritage, 1967), a beautifully mounted illustrated history of the Elizabethan Age, and Neville Williams's *The Life and Times of Elizabeth I* (New York: Doubleday, 1972).

Peggy K. Liss, *Isabel the Queen: Life and Times*. New York: Oxford University Press, 1992. This is a masterful biography of the famous Spanish monarch, which not only covers her best-known exploit—sponsoring Columbus's initial voyage—but also reveals her less well known and not so admirable acts, including her strong support of the Spanish Inquisition and persecution of Spanish Jews. Also see Nancy Rubin's *Isabella of Castile: The First Renaissance Queen* (New York: St. Martin's Press, 1991), another admirable portrait of Isabella.

Golda Meir, *My Life*. New York: G. P. Putnam's Sons, 1975. In this autobiography Meir tells about her eventful childhood and adolescence, her marriage and immigration to Palestine in the 1920s, and her stints as Israel's labor minister, foreign minister, and prime minister. She also reveals her feelings about Israel's right to exist and what must be done to ensure its survival. A more recent, and arguably less biased, account is *Golda Meir: The Romantic Years* (New York: Scribner's, 1988), by the prolific biographer Ralph G. Martin, which chronicles her life through the founding of the Israeli state in 1948.

Margaret Thatcher, *The Downing Street Years*. New York: Harper-Collins, 1993. "The Iron Lady" delivers a powerful personal account of her years as Britain's prime minister, including anecdotes about her election victories, the Falkland Islands crisis, and the various national and international leaders she knew and with whom she negotiated. A more comprehensive view of Thatcher's whole life is found in Hugo Young's biography *The Iron Lady* (New York: Farrar, Straus, Giroux, 1989).

Primary Sources:

Leon Bernard and Theodore B. Hodges, eds., *Readings in European History*. New York: Macmillan, 1958.

Julius Caesar, *Commentaries on the Gallic and Civil Wars*, published as *War Commentaries of Caesar*. Trans. Rex Warner. New York: New American Library, 1960.

Baldesar Castiglione, *The Book of the Courtier*. Trans. Charles S. Singleton. New York: Doubleday, 1959.

Catherine II, *Memoirs*. Trans. Moura Budberg, ed. Dominique Maroger. New York: Macmillan, 1961.

Dio Cassius, *Roman History*, excerpted in *The Roman History: The Reign of Augustus*. Trans. Ian Scott-Kilvert. New York: Penguin Books, 1987.

Herodotus, *The Histories*. Trans. Aubrey de Sélincourt. New York: Penguin Books, 1972.

Plutarch, *Lives of the Noble Grecians and Romans*. Trans. John Dryden. New York: Random House, 1932; also excerpted in *Fall of the Roman Republic: Six Lives by Plutarch*. Trans. Rex Warner. New York: Penguin Books, 1972; and *Makers of Rome: Nine Lives by Plutarch*. Trans. Ian Scott-Kilvert. New York: Penguin Books, 1965.

William Safire, ed., *Lend Me Your Ears: Great Speeches in History*. New York: W. W. Norton, 1997.

Suetonius, *Lives of the Twelve Caesars*, published as *The Twelve Caesars*. Trans. Robert Graves, rev. Michael Grant. New York: Penguin Books, 1979.

Tacitus, *Annals*. Trans. Michael Grant. New York: Penguin Books, 1989.

Eugen Weber, ed., *The Western Tradition: From the Ancient World to Louis XIV*. Boston: D. C. Heath, 1965.

Secondary Sources:

Katherine Anthony, *Queen Elizabeth*. New York: Knopf, 1929.

J. P. V. D. Balsdon, *Roman Women: Their History and Habits*. Westport, CT: Greenwood Press, 1975.

Elizabeth Barber, *Women's Work: The First 20,000 Years*. New York: W. W. Norton, 1994.

Mary R. Beard, *Women as a Force in History*. New York: Octagon Books, 1967.

S. T. Bindoff, *Tudor England*. Baltimore: Penguin Books, 1966.

Daniel J. Boorstin, *The Discoverers*. New York: Random House, 1985.

Ernle Bradford, *Cleopatra*. New York: Harcourt, Brace, Jovanovich, 1972.

Catherine Bush, *Elizabeth I*. New York: Chelsea House, 1985.

Robert Coughlan, *Elizabeth and Catherine, Empresses of All the Russias*. New York: G. P. Putnam's Sons, 1974.

Will Durant, *The Age of Faith*. New York: Simon and Schuster, 1950.

———, *The Reformation*. New York: Simon and Schuster, 1957.

George Gardiner, *Margaret Thatcher: From Childhood to Leadership*. London: William Kimber, 1975.

Bernard Garfinkel, *Margaret Thatcher*. New York: Chelsea House, 1985.

Edward Gibbon, *The Decline and Fall of the Roman Empire*. 3 vols. Ed. David Womersley. New York: Penguin Books, 1994.

Frances and Joseph Gies, *Women in the Middle Ages*. New York: Crowell, 1978.

Peter Green, *Alexander to Actium: The Historical Evolution of the Hellenistic Age*. Berkeley and Los Angeles: University of California Press, 1990.

Christopher Hibbert, *Daily Life in Victorian England*. New York: American Heritage, 1975.

———, *The Story of England*. London: Phaidon, 1992.

Penny Junor, *Margaret Thatcher: Wife, Mother, Politician*. London: Sidgwick, 1983.

Vicki Leon, *Uppity Women of Ancient Times*. Berkeley, CA: Conari Press, 1995.

———, *Uppity Women of Medieval Times*. Berkeley, CA: Conari Press, 1997.

Naphtali Lewis, *Life in Egypt Under Roman Rule*. Oxford, England: Clarendon Press, 1983.

Karen McAuley, *Golda Meir*. New York: Chelsea House, 1985.

Melveena McKendrick, *Ferdinand and Isabella*. New York: Harper and Row, 1968.

Kenneth O. Morgan, ed., *The Oxford Illustrated History of Britain*. New York: Oxford University Press, 1986.

Sarah B. Pomeroy, *Goddesses, Whores, Wives, and Slaves: Women in Classical Antiquity*. New York: Shocken Books, 1995.

Nicholas V. Riasanovsky, *A History of Russia*. New York: Oxford University Press, 1984.

Robert Slater, *Golda: The Uncrowned Queen of Israel*. New York: Jonathan David, 1981.

Lytton Strachey, *Queen Victoria*. New York: Harcourt, Brace, 1921.

Henry C. Watson, *Heroic Women of History*. Philadelphia: John Potter, 1931.

Colin Wells, *The Roman Empire*. London: Fontana, 1992.

INDEX

absolutism, 10, 27
Academy of Sciences, 57
Adolphus, Gustavus (king of Sweden),
    22
Agrippa, Marcus, 33
Albert (prince of Saxe-Coburg), 63–64,
    65
Alekseyevna, Yekaterina. *See* Catherine
    II (queen of Russia)
Alexander the Great, 26
Alfonso V (king of Portugal), 39
Amal magazine, 89
Amazonomachy, 12
Amazons, 12, 17, 24
Anhalt-Zerbst, Sophie Friederike
    Auguste von. *See* Catherine II (queen
    of Russia)
Anthony, Katherine, 51
anti-Semitism, 69
Antonius, Marcus (Mark Antony), 15,
    25, 30–31
    death of, 34
    defeat of, 33
Argentina, 10
Armada. *See* Spanish Armada
Artemisia (queen of Caria), 15
Ascham, Roger, 46
Assyrian Empire, 14–15
Astor, Lady, 24
Athens, 12
Auletes. *See* Ptolemy XII (king of
    Egypt)
Aurelian, 19

Balfour Declaration, 71
Balfour, Arthur, 71
"bedchamber crisis," 63
Ben-Gurion, David, 73
Berenice, 27
Bhutto, Ali (father), 84–85, 88
Bhutto, Benazir (prime minister of
    Pakistan), 10, 23
    dismissal of, 90, 91
    education at Oxford University, 87
    education at Radcliffe College, 87
    election to prime minister of, 89–90,
        91
    execution of father and, 88

imprisonment of, 88
obstacles of, 84
reforms and, 90–91
restoration of democracy and, 90
returns to Lahore (Pakistan), 89
social privileges of, 86
visits foreign nations, 87
Bhutto, Mir (brother), 86
Bhutto, Nusrat (mother), 86
Bhutto, Sanam (sister), 86
Bhutto, Shah (brother), 86
Bhutto, Shah Nawaz (grandfather), 86
Boleyn, Anne (mother of Elizabeth I), 46
Bosporus Strait, 58
Boudicca, 18, 83
Britain. *See* England
Brown, John, 65–67
burqa, 86

Caesar, Julius, 9, 18, 25, 27, 28
    death of, 30
Caesarion. *See* Ptolemy XV
Canossa, House of, 20
Cardel, Babbete, 53
Caria (Asia minor), 15
Castile, 8, 22
Catherine II (queen of Russia), 10, 23
    Academy of Sciences of, 57
    Charter of the Nobility of, 57
    coronation of, 54
    credo of, 56–57
    death of, 59
    education of, 53
    Enlightenment and, 55–57
    faults of, 53
    foreign policy of, 58
    Free Economic Society of, 57
    Legislative Commission of, 55
    personal affairs of, 59
    Peter III and, 53–54
    qualities of, 52
    reforms of, 54–55
    State Bank of, 57
    Translators' Commission of, 57
Catherine the Great. *See* Catherine II
    (queen of Russia)
Catholic Church, 22, 40, 42, 46–47, 49
Cecil, Sir William, 47

108

Phillip II (king of Spain), 50
Poalei Zion (Labor Zionist Party), 72
Pompey, Gnaeus, 28–29
Potemkin, Grigory, 59
Pothinus, 28–29
prime ministers, 23
protectorates, 27
Ptolemaic dynasty, 9
Ptolemy XII (king of Egypt), 26, 27
Ptolemy XIII (brother of Cleopatra
 VII), 28–29
Ptolemy XIV (brother of Cleopatra
 VII), 30
Ptolemy XV (son of Cleopatra VII), 30
Pulgar, Hernando del, 8

Raleigh, Sir Walter, 48
religious-political conflicts, 22, 46, 49
Riasanovsky, Nicholas, 52
Roberts, Alfred, 77–78
Roman Empire, 27
 civil war of, 28
Russia, 10, 23
 Enlightenment and, 55–57
 reforms in, 54–55
 transformed by Catherine II and, 52

Sammuramat (queen of Assyria),
 14–15, 17
Santa Hermandad, 39–40
Scythians, 12–13
Second Triumvirate, 30–31
Semiramide (Rossini), 15
Semiramis. *See* Sammuramat (queen of
 Assyria)
Senate House, 30
Seymour, Edward, 46
Seymour, Jane, 46
Shakespeare, William, 44
Shamshi-Adad V (king of Assyria), 14
Sharif, Nawaz, 91
Smith, Lacey B., 48
Spain
 conquest of Granada by, 42
 economic reforms of Isabella I and,
  39–40
 unification of, 35, 37–38
 war with Portugal, 39
Spanish Armada, 9, 50
Spanish Inquisition, 22, 40–42
State Bank, 57
steppes, 11–12
Stettin (Germany), 53

Stuart, Mary. *See* Mary (queen of Scots)

Tacitus, 18
Tarsus (Asia Minor), 31
term limits, 23
Thatcher, Denis (husband), 78
Thatcher, Margaret (prime minister of
 England), 10, 23
 achievements of, 76
 Denis Thatcher and, 78
 economic unrest and, 80–81
 education at Oxford University, 78
 Falklands War and, 81–83
 "the Iron Lady," 80
 principles of, 80
 qualities of, 76–77
 resigns as prime minister, 76, 83
Thirty Years' War, 22
Tomyris (queen of Caria), 15
Translators' Commission, 57–58
Tudor, House of, 46
Tudor, Mary. *See* Mary I (queen of
 England)
Tudor, Edward. *See* Edward VI (king of
 England)

Ulrich, Peter. *See* Peter III (king of
 Russia)

Victoria (queen of England), 10, 23
 accedes to the throne, 60
 Albert (prince of Saxe-Coburg),
  63–65
 "bedchamber crisis" of, 63
 death of, 67
 death of Albert and, 65
 "the Grandmother of Europe," 64
 John Brown and, 65–67
 Lord Melbourne and, 63
 morals of, 60
 political neutrality of, 63
 transforms the monarchy, 61
Victorian Age, 60

women
 mystical attributes of, 17, 24
 traditional roles of, 12
 traditional view of, 8

Yom Kippur War, 75
Young, Hugo, 76, 77

Zenobia (queen of Palmyra), 19–20

PICTURE CREDITS

ABOUT THE AUTHOR

Historian and award-winning writer Don Nardo has published many volumes of both single and multiple biography, among them *Julius Caesar, Thomas Jefferson, Charles Darwin, John Wayne, H. G. Wells, Franklin D. Roosevelt,* and *Rulers of Ancient Rome.* Mr. Nardo also writes screenplays and teleplays and composes music. He resides on Cape Cod, Massachusetts, with his wife, Christine, who conceived the idea of and contributed many valuable insights to this unique volume on noteworthy women leaders.